FAITH IN THE NEIGHBORHOOD
UNDERSTANDING AMERICA'S RELIGIOUS DIVERSITY

VOLUME THREE

Loss

FAITH IN THE NEIGHBORHOOD
UNDERSTANDING AMERICA'S RELIGIOUS DIVERSITY

VOLUME THREE

LOSS

LUCINDA MOSHER

SEABURY BOOKS
An imprint of Church Publishing, Incorporated
New York

In memoriam
Gurcharan Singh, Ph.D.
1930 – 2007

Published in the United States of America by Church Publishing,
Incorporated. No portion of this book may be reproduced, stored in or
introduced into a retrieval system, or transmitted, in any form or by any
means—including photocopying—without the prior written permission of
Church Publishing, except in the case of brief quotations embedded in critical articles and reviews.

Library of Congress Cataloging-in-Publication Data
Mosher, Lucinda.
Loss / by Lucinda Mosher.
    p.   cm. — (Faith in the neighborhood)
Includes bibliographical references.
ISBN 978-1-59627-059-6 (pbk.)
    1. Suffering—Religious aspects. 2. Loss (Psychology)—Religious aspects.
3. Death—Religious aspects. 4. Spirituality. I. Title.
BL65.S85M67 2007
202'.2—dc22   2007028841

Printed in the United States of America.

Church Publishing, Incorporated
445 Fifth Avenue
New York, New York 10016
www.churchpublishing.org

Contents

Acknowledgments

THE IDEA FOR THE *Faith in the Neighborhood* series came from Cynthia Shattuck, my editor. Thus once again, hearty thanks go to her for her brainstorm and her continuing guidance. As always, profound gratitude is due to Barrie Mosher, my husband and dearest friend, for technological assistance—and cheerleading.

Research support was provided by the Trinity Grants Program at Trinity Church–St. Paul's Chapel (New York City). I am grateful to the Trinity Church vestry, not just for this, but also for their ongoing enthusiasm for the *Faith in the Neighborhood* series. I am thankful also to New York Disaster Interfaith Services for research facilitation.

Thanks are due to the Reverend Daniel Appleyard, Professor Claude Jacobs, and everyone associated with the annual *Worldviews Seminar* in Dearborn, Michigan. Particular thanks go to Kersey Antia, Ph.D., Zoroastrian High Priest of Chicago, Illinois; Rabbi Tzvi Blanchard, Ph.D., CLAL (The National Jewish Center for Learning and Leadership); Timothy Cahill, Ph.D., Loyola University New Orleans; Faroque Khan, M.D., MACP, State University of New York at Stony Brook; Laurie Patton, Ph.D., Emory University; Marianne Tanabe, M.D., University of Hawai'i; and David Zuniga (Dae-il Sunim), Hospice Austin—all of whom shared instructional materials, lecture notes, articles, or research findings with me. Arvind

Vora provided research assistance, as did Millicent Browne. Dr. Lynne Boyle, producer of Detroit Public Television's award-winning *Interfaith Odyssey,* allowed me to excerpt a number of episodes. Grove Harris critiqued an early draft. This book is richer for their generosity.

Having taught about the world's religions and America's religious diversity for many years, my way of explaining things cannot help but borrow from many sources. Where I use the ideas of others in *Faith in the Neighborhood,* I do so with great respect and a deep sense of indebtedness. However, the responsibility for any factual or conceptual errors rests with me.

Since the inception of the *Faith in the Neighborhood* project, I have been able to count on support from the Long Island Multi-Faith Forum. Just as I completed this volume, I received word of the death of Dr. Gurcharan Singh, a founding member of the Forum. I knew him to be a devout Sikh, a fine scholar, a gracious interviewee, and an elegant practitioner of positive interreligious relations in the challenging environment of post-9/11 Greater New York City. My hope is that this book might honor Professor Singh's memory in some small way.

Lucinda Mosher
Palm Sunday 2007

Series Preface

AS THE FLOODWATERS began to recede, an urgent aspect of the Recovery Phase of the Federal Emergency Management Agency's response to Hurricane Katrina and its aftermath was the retrieval of victims' bodies. According to news reports, a chaplain accompanied each four-person retrieval team FEMA deployed. When a body was located, the chaplain was to offer an "ecumenical" prayer, even before the required documentation of the remains and their surroundings was performed. Bodies were then transported under police escort to a Disaster Portable Morgue Unit, where again a chaplain would pray over the remains. Finally, after all record-making was completed, the morgue staff was to perform a ceremonial washing of each corpse, which (so FEMA authorities thought) would comply with Jewish, Christian, and Muslim requirements for preparing a body for burial.

The goal of these efforts was to accord dignity and respect to each victim of a national tragedy. This was noble enough, and even comforting for many people to hear. However, it also raised a number of questions. Who decided what made a prayer "ecumenical"? Could any single washing ceremony truly comply with the requirements of several different religions? Those who lost their lives to Hurricane Katrina and the subsequent flood included Buddhists, Sikhs, Hindus, followers of Afro-Caribbean religions, and more. Had any of this government-sponsored praying and washing taken that into consideration? Truly Hurricane Katrina brings into focus the multireligious implications of catastrophic loss in twenty-first-century America.

In this third volume of the *Faith in the Neighborhood* series, we investigate understandings of destiny, loss, death, and remembrance in multireligious America. We will learn from followers of certain Afro-Caribbean and Native American traditions, Buddhists, Hindus, Jains, Jews, Muslims, Sikhs, Zoroastrians, Shinto-followers, Taoists, and members of the Bahá'í Faith. We listen in as nurses, physicians, chaplains, religious leaders, morticians, educators, and many others wrestle with questions such as: Why are we here, and what is our destiny? What causes illness? How can our religion guide us in making decisions about certain kinds of medical treatment options? What religion-related issues would it be helpful for a healthcare provider to know? What happens when we die? Therefore, what should happen to the body of the deceased? How shall we manage our grief?

In Chapter 1, "What We Are," we think about what it means to be a *person*. We learn about attitudes toward the physical body and its relationship to the soul (or self, as some prefer to say), and how some of the religions in America's neighborhoods explain what happens when we die. Chapter 2, "When We're Ailing," investigates attitudes toward illness, healthcare, and hospitalization. Chapter 3, "Postponing Death, Extending Life," explores how our neighbors draw upon the principles of their religion as they opt for, or reject, use of life-extending technology, organ transplantation, and organ donation. Chapter 4, "Transition," helps us understand some of the religious rituals performed when the death of a loved one is imminent and in the moments after death has come. We learn how funerals are conducted in some of America's religions: how the remains are handled, and what we might expect if we are invited to attend. Chapter 5, "Recovery," investigates how our neighbors' religions facilitate the grieving process.

Method and Approach

Faith in the Neighborhood is for Christians who, having begun to notice the religious complexity of their neighborhoods, are both curious and ready to dig below the surface to understand their neighbors as they understand themselves. It encourages the reader to become, as Martin Forward puts it, "theologically and religiously multilingual." This is an authentic Christian endeavor because, as Jesus reminds us, we are to love our neighbor as ourselves. Furthermore, the Ninth Commandment prohibits us from bearing false witness against our neighbor. Certainly, the more we know about our neighbor's concepts, categories, and vocabulary, the better we can bear truthful witness regarding our neighbor's religious beliefs and practices.

In American life today, various religions intertwine (or collide) in the factory, the office suite, the boardroom, the classroom, the shopping mall, the sidewalk, the street fair, the city park, the potluck supper—and even in our own homes. *Faith in the Neighborhood* is for the reader who prefers to listen to the voices of America's many religions as they glide in and out of the narrative—just as they do in real life. And, when *Faith in the Neighborhood* speaks of "America," it is following the example of scholars who use the term as shorthand for "within the U.S.A.," all the while acknowledging that "America" is more than a single country.

It is difficult to do justice to the wide variety and nuance within each religion. As anyone who has ever tried to teach an introductory course in Christianity can tell you, no matter what Christian custom you name, and no matter how you describe its meaning, someone will raise a hand to protest, "But in my church, we don't do it that way"; or, "But in my church, we don't call it that"; or "But in my church, that's not what it means." Think of baptism and communion—Christianity's most basic rites. Among Christians, each are performed and explained in more than one way. Likewise, as anyone engaged in Christian ecumenical efforts will attest, and as many of us know from our daily interactions in our own neighborhoods, the intra-Christian conversation is complex, sometimes heated, and often confusing—especially to the outsider.

We need to keep this in mind as we hear about Hindu, Buddhist, Jewish, or Muslim ways of doing things. We all have a tendency to speak or write of "the Buddhist community in Los Angeles," or "the Jewish community in Texas," or "America's Hindu community." This blurs the fact that these are blanket terms covering quite a swath of diversity. As our conversation proceeds, sometimes one branch or school of thought will be given the floor; at other times, another. In the end, a range of voices will have had a chance to speak. Whichever religion we're talking about at the moment, somewhere in America there is a family, a congregation, a community who does things or talks about things a little differently. The descriptions and interpretations of doctrines, rituals, and customs in this short book are representative, but not exhaustive. So don't be surprised if your neighbor says, "That's not how I'd put it," or "We don't do it that way at all!" Rather, enjoy the opportunity to say, "Well then, please tell me how you *do* think about these things, and please help me understand why."

All quotations come from real conversations in many parts of the United States. Unless noted, all speakers do practice the religion about which they are speaking. An effort has been made to balance "ordinary adherents" with "highly trained religious leaders," women with men, and older people with younger. A short book can only hint at the range of attitudes and understandings, so some perspectives may be unreported. Indeed, dozens of religions in the American multifaith landscape are not even mentioned! Yet that is part of the point: these books invite you to overhear a conversation so that you might initiate one of your own. The discussion need never end.

Series Resources

Becoming religiously multilingual requires that we learn new words from many languages. The appendix of this book has a glossary to remind you of definitions, along with a very basic outline of each religion, and suggestions for further reading.

CHAPTER ONE

What We Are

WHERE DO WE COME FROM? *What Are We? Where Are We Going?* These questions, which seem to have been influenced by the Christian catechism he studied as a boy, are the title of a famous painting by Paul Gauguin. Against a lush Tahitian landscape, the artist has placed birds and animals, a carved statue, and a number of human figures (elderly, very young, and in between) in tableaus that invite us to consider the relationship of human beings to each other, to the natural order, and to the transcendent.

The questions illustrated in Gauguin's painting are *worldview questions*—questions to which religions provide answers. They lead in turn to other questions—about things such as the nature of illness and the appropriate response to loss. America's expanding multireligiousness means that a variety of worldview *answers* live side by side in our neighborhoods, informing our neighbors' healthcare concerns, their customs regarding death, and their approaches to grieving and remembrance. It means that we may be summoned to the funeral of a friend who is Jain, or Sikh, or Muslim. We may want to know what to expect ritually, but we will appreciate more fully what we see if we first take a moment to consider what our neighbors' religions have to say about what Gauguin has asked. It is best, however, to start with his second question, *What are we?*

———————

What Are We?

In a famous episode of "Star Trek: The Next Generation," Data, a highly intelligent (albeit robotic) member of the starship crew, is to become the subject of a scientist's experiment. Aware that the scientist's research may well destroy him, Data decides to avoid the risk by resigning from Starfleet. But, the eager scientist counters, Data *cannot* resign his commission! One must be a person to do this, and Data is not a *person;* he is merely "a piece of Starfleet property." To save Data, Captain Piccard must prove that Data is indeed a sentient being; that he is indeed self-aware; that he measures up to the accepted definition of *personhood.*

Exactly how personhood is defined undergirds our neighbors' concepts of where we come from and what happens when we die. Medical ethics specialists tell us it is key to deciding who is worthy of moral respect. Religious leaders know it plays a role in helping families address a wide range of medical concerns. It also is at the basis of funeral and memorial practices. This is why we will consider it first. So, what *are* we?

We are body and soul
"Jewish approaches to things are always attempting to negotiate tensions that are irresolvable," offers Rabbi Tzvi Blanchard, of the National Jewish Center for Learning and Leadership. "To be human is to negotiate irresolvable tensions. There is a classic Jewish notion that a *person* is composed of body and soul." In a Jewish psychology of personhood, he continues, "there are perceptions and knowledge; there is story; there are memories. You're a *person* if you have those. If you've lost all your memory—if you don't remember any of it, if you couldn't in principle remember any of it—what does it mean to call yourself a

person?" Jews have also defined personhood in terms of moral responsibility, he notes, and this too is supported by the classical texts. "Persons are capable of understanding norms and responding to them. God speaks to Adam and Eve and tells them, 'Don't do this.' That's what separates personhood from animalhood."

From a Christian biblical perspective, Frederick Buechner asserts, it is not that a human is a being that *has* a body; rather, he insists, a human being *is* a body. "When God made Adam, he did it by slapping some mud together to make a body and then breathing some breath into it to make a living soul. Thus the body and soul…are as inextricably part and parcel of each other as the leaves and flames that make up a bonfire."[1] Buechner is drawing on the second chapter of Genesis. Christians often point to Genesis's first chapter, and assert that a human is a being made "in God's image and after God's likeness."

We are part of Great Life
"We don't agree with you," a Mohawk leader comments. "That's too narrow. The deer is also made in the image of God. So is the bear, the eagle, the snake, the frog, the trees, the grass, water. All life reflects God." His attitude is echoed by members of some of America's other First Nations. "We see ourselves as part of what we call the Great Life," says Dawi Wistona, a *didahnawisgi*—a traditional healer. At times, he speaks of himself as Cherokee; at others, as Keetoowah. Both names have their place, he explains: "I see myself as a person of Cherokee ancestry following Keetoowah traditions." By whichever name, he says, "we see people as alive, plants as alive, animals as alive, stones as alive; the water is alive, the fire is alive, the earth is alive. So, when you say 'a person,' I ask: what kind of 'person' are we talking about? Are we talking about a two-legged person? A four-legged person? A person with wings? A person who is a stone? To us, these are *all* living beings that have personhood. If we are talking about two-legged people, we believe that we were the last thing created. We are the last; we are the least—not the greatest, not the pinnacle of creation. Every species has its gift, and one is not necessarily more important than the others."

"To take it a little bit further," he continues, "I would say that we believe that, as two-legged animals, it is our job in life to *become* a human being. It is a conscious process. You have to choose it, and you have to work at it. Human beings are the only animals that have the ability to alter their nature. You never see a deer deciding, 'You know, I am so tired of being a deer; today, I'm going to act like a chipmunk.' Humans have a choice. We can just do what we need to do to serve our own needs; or, we can choose something more than that. That's up to us. Cherokee people will often refer to themselves as *ani-yvwiya*— which means anybody who is a *real* person. A *real* person is a person of heart, a person of spirit, a person who lives a life of love and service. It's interesting. One of my elders says that to be a Keetoowah, you have to be Christ-like."

Put another way, "Humans are beings that have been put on this earth with only four things to do," says a Keetoowah activist. "One is to take care of each other; one is to take care of all of creation; one is to give thanks; and (in a good way) one is to take care of ourselves. If we do those four things, we are pretty much complete people."

"We Keetoowahs believe that the human acquisition of consciousness was so traumatic," Dawi Wistona explains, "that it actually shattered our spirits into two parts: *adanado,* the heart; and *udayvladv,* the shadow. They are in competition with each other, because they are not connected. Each one is vying for control and power. Each one has strengths and weaknesses. True human beings are those who examine their heart and get to know it inside and out, those who examine their shadow and get to know it inside and out. By doing that, we start to weave these two aspects of ourselves back together to create a sort of tapestry—someone who has the heart to moderate the qualities of the shadow which are not that positive, and who has the strength of the shadow to give the heart more power. That, to us, is a human being."

The Cherokee speak of Great Life; similarly, Shinto-followers speak of Great Nature. Human beings are "Children of Divine Nature," as one Shinto priest puts it. Each of us is *wake-mitama,* an individual manifestation of the divine, a holy being who is developing into a *kami.* Shinto emphasizes purification, one young musician reminds us. "When we say 'purify,' we mean all parts of us—our body and our mind and our spirit. We don't think of them separately."

And, similar to the Cherokee notion of the human being as a tapestry of heart and shadow, a Taoist sees the human being as the meeting place of heaven and earth. Taoism lacks the notion of a soul in the Christian sense, a *Qigong* master explains. Rather, Taoism speaks of our matrix of *hun* and *p'o*. A person has three *hun*, entities which, some say, rest in the liver; and seven *p'o*—which, some say, rest in the lungs. *Hun* is the *yang* dimension: spirit, intellect; the person's light, heavenly, ongoing aspect. *P'o* is the *yin* dimension: physical vitality; the person's earthly, dark aspect. But there is another way to think about it, he suggests. The ancient Chinese pictogram for *ren*, which means "person," has just two strokes. These are two legs, "and that's it!" he explains. "A person is bi-pedal, an animal that walks on two legs."

We are our ancestors
In the Afro-Atlantic traditions, a Vodou priest tells us, "part of what defines our personhood is the fact that we have a *Mèt Tèt*, a deity who owns our head. Our destiny is defined by the deities. This, along with the ancestral knowledge that literally inhabits us, defines the life of the mind. And when I say 'my ancestors,' I mean that *personhood* is defined beyond who and what we think we are in *this* space and time. Actually, it's an accumulation of the knowledge, the histories, of people from the past, coming from beyond. A problem in the past can be visited on *you*, and you will have to remedy that, no matter what. I might do it by means of a rite where I literally feed the earth. I make a huge hole in the ground and I make offerings, I pour libations, I make foods, I give the *ashé* of something to the earth, and that will remedy things."

Consciousness is part of personhood, she continues. Vodou teaches that "one's consciousness has two aspects. You have your *ti-bon-zanj* and your *gwo-bon-zanj:* your 'little good angel' and your 'big good angel.' Your *gwo-bon-zanj* is essentially the breath of life—the breath of *your* life. It's what would be your soul or your spirit. The *ti-bon-zanj* would be the more rational, day-to-day, intuitive, emotional, mental responses that we have to the world."

We are agents of God
A Zoroastrian might say that personhood has three aspects: the *urvan*—individuality, or soul; the *fravashi*—the divine essence within us; and *tanu*—the physical body. "There is something more," says Professor K. Dinshah Irani, Professor Emeritus of Philosophy at New York's City College. "We are rational creatures—able to grasp our experience of the world, but also able to recognize mentally what the ideal world should be. We can see *asha*, the ideal truth. Once we grasp *asha*, it becomes our inclination to promote it and establish it as best as we can. This is Good Thought. When we articulate that in the context in which we affect others, that is Good Word. And when we reflect on it, we act. So there is no such thing as a Good Deed without Good Thought, because nothing is prescribed as such. You have to think it out in each context, and maximize the ideal."

"A *person* is an agent of God on this earth," explains Dr. Kersey Antia, a Chicago priest. "We are supposed to do everything that God is supposed to do. In the *Gathas,* our earliest scripture, it says: 'Whichever way God has made himself a wise and righteous ruler, let us emulate that within our own self and give it back in full measure.' As an agent of God, a person has to bring *frashokereti,* which means 'renovation of the world.' In the *Gathas* it says: 'May we be those who carry out the *frashokereti* for you, O Ahura Mazda.' Two or three days ago, I happened to hear Oprah Winfrey saying, 'Before I die, I want to do this; I want to do that.' And I said, 'Here goes a Zoroastrian!' She is trying to do whatever good she can, and bring whatever good she can in this world. That is the Zoroastrian spirit."

We are a soul in a body
From an Islamic perspective, says a professor of medicine, a human being is a soul in a body, created to serve God. "The Qur'an tells us that God breathes into us his breath, his *ruh*," notes Imam Yusuf Hasan, a chaplain at Memorial Sloan Kettering Cancer Center. "God's *ruh* never dies. The human being is the character of a person, not the physical body which

goes back to the earth. That's why we Muslims take names that have meaning. My name is Yusuf, which means *beloved*. My last name is Hasan, *one that makes better, one who improves on things*. So a Muslim has this character to develop. That helps us. Words make people." Muslims often speak of God's Beautiful Names—descriptions of God drawn from the Qur'an and the Tradition, like The Compassionate, The Just, The Patient—and many more. From an Islamic perspective, humans are mirrors of God's attributes, and should strive to reflect as many as possible.

We are soul

"We are soul," says a Bahá'í social worker. "Bahá'ís believe that the world of the womb prepares that soul, that person, for the material world. And so, in the womb, that human being is developing what it needs to survive in this world. Bahá'u'lláh, the founder of the Bahá'í Faith, teaches that this world is characterized by tests and difficulties. A grain of sand or an irritant gets into the oyster, and that irritation creates a beautiful pearl. Our soul is like that. Through the tests and difficulties of this life, a beautiful gem is created. Bahá'u'lláh says that human beings are like a mine filled with gems of inestimable value; and that education alone is what helps those gems to manifest themselves. And so, in this world, we're developing our spiritual arms, legs, eyes, and ears because the soul will continue to progress through different spiritual worlds (which he says are countless in number) that we really don't know *about*, but know *of*."

We are atman

For Jains and Hindus, a *person* is an *atman* in a body. Many Jains in America translate *atman* as "soul." "While we are alive, the soul is present in every sense of the body," a Jain biochemist explains. "The body is in constant change, and disintegrates in the long run. The body will change, no matter what; the soul remains constant. So we have to focus on the soul, which is non-changing. We are to get in touch with our soul, learn more about soul, help the soul be rid of any bad *karmas*." Birth in the human body can provide access to the destiny of release. "Only the human can think and can change the way of thinking and the way of living," says an internist. "The shedding of bad *karma*, the getting rid of bad *karma* will work only in the human," a pediatrician elaborates. Once an *atman* is born as a human, is it always born as a human after that? "No," she says. "We can go backwards. Anything can happen."

Some Hindus are comfortable translating *atman* as "soul," but others are not. "I think *soul* has too many Christian connotations," one philosopher explains, "so I usually use the word *self*. It points to something similar, but it prevents any association with a Christian notion of original sin." Personhood comes more from the *atman* than the body it inhabits, but the body is not unimportant, a nephrologist remarks. "We Hindus have our own ancient system of *ayurvedic* medicine. *Ayurveda* means knowledge concerning life in this body of ours. My religion teaches me to take a personal rather than a businesslike approach to my patient, and to treat him as a whole. The body is a whole system. I specialize in kidneys. But the kidneys are not separate from the heart or the lungs. They are all interrelated. You can treat one, but you have to consider everything else involved, because everything interacts."

In another sense, a traditional reading of the Hindu sacred texts would have us believe that "one does not become a 'person' until one has all of the right initiation rituals," explains Professor Deepak Sarma of Case Western Reserve University. For a *Brahmin* boy, this is the Sacred Thread ceremony, performed around eleven years of age. While it is becoming increasingly common to hold this ceremony in American temples, many families still prefer to take their sons to India for this important occasion. "So, in a sense," he notes, "many American Hindus go back to India to become a 'person.'"

We are jiva

"To be honest with you, I don't think there is such a thing as *soul*," says a Sikh professor. "I think *soul* is a very Jewish-Christian term. I don't see it in Sikh scripture at all. In Sikhism, a dichotomy of body and soul is an alien concept. The better term is *jiva*, life. That's what it is." As she sees it, *soul* may not be an authentically Sikh term, but *self* is. "There are many layers to the self: the body; the senses; the mind; the intellect; the spirit. They are all beautiful, but you are an integrated person, not body versus soul." From a Sikh perspective, "the body is very good. We love God with every pore! Every little hair of mine desires the Divine One. The body is a temple of the Divine One. The body contains the divine spark. So we should respect our bodies and everyone else's bodies."

We are a body-mind continuum
"The definition that existed at the time of the Buddha was that there is this unchanging, everlasting entity within each person," a Theravada monk explains. "In listening to that, the Buddha said, 'I do not see such a thing.' The Buddha denied a self or soul—the *atman*. He denied that concept."

"I am mindful that sometimes Buddhists do use the term *soul*," remarks a Zen hospital chaplain in Texas, "but I discourage that because it goes against almost all Buddhist thought. This is perhaps the single biggest difference between Buddhism and all other religions. In Buddhism, there is no soul—that is, no permanent, fixed, eternal, individual entity in us. We believe we are all interconnected, and we are all compilations of other elements, such as DNA, social trends, past experiences, consciousness, and more."

The term *soul* simply does not express Buddhist teaching adequately, says a Zen priest in Chicago. "In Buddhism, the primary teaching is *anatman* (which is a Sanskrit term) or *anatta* (its equivalent in the Pali dialect). Whichever term you use, it means 'no self'; it means 'there is no soul.' *Body-mind* or *body-mind-soul* are false divisions. There's nothing separate, nothing that separates 'me' from 'you.' We are interconnected. There is only the appearance, the provisional sense of separation. I am here and you are there, but we are really just this mind. We are all this mind. We cannot be just a piece of it."

"I am aware that some Christians are offended when they hear Buddhists speak of 'no-soul,' says a member of Wisconsin's Tibetan Buddhist community. "However, this does not mean there is no continuity of 'being.' In our tradition, at least, it means that there is no 'absolute, independent, autonomous existence.' We would say that a *person* is 'a body-mind continuum." From the Tibetan Buddhist perspective, we could also describe a *human person* as a cluster of four or five psychophysical aspects, he suggests.

Actually, says Geshe Lhundub Sopa, founder of Wisconsin's Deer Park Buddhist Center, this is true of all beings in the realms of cyclic existence, animals included, as well as all beings that are free from cyclic existence, such as Buddhas. "For a human, the lifetime begins when, due to *karma,* the subtle consciousness joins with the combined sperm and egg in the mother's womb," he explains. "In reality, a person is changing from moment to moment within a given lifetime. Though the name is the same from moment to moment, the person's psycho-physical aspects are in constant flux."

Look at it this way, Geshe-la suggests: "That to which we attribute personhood—let us say, 'Frank,' for example—is like the month 'September.' Is 'September' the first day, the third day, the thirtieth? We can't say. 'September' is a label we put on a series of thirty days. 'September' does not exist separate from those days, nor is it any one of those days, nor is any one of the days 'September.' In the same way, not only is Frank's existence dependent on his psycho-physical constituents in each moment, it is also dependent on the continuum of moments that make up his lifetime." In short, "a person exists only dependently. That is, *a person* is empty of absolute, independent, autonomous existence."

Finally, a Zen practitioner notes, "in Buddhist teaching, only the human can gain enlightenment. Only a *person* can take responsibility for his or her own actions. Basically, a *person* is one whose job is to move farther along the path towards enlightenment."

Where Do We Come From?

Given these teachings about personhood, how would we answer the question, "Where have we come from?" Have we spilled forth from, or are we a manifestation of, some ultimate source? Are we the product of a Creator's intention? Or, have we simply always been?

"We believe that we come from the east when we are born into the world," says an Ojibway administrator. "We come from the *kami*-realm, the realm of the deities," says a Shinto priest. "We receive our life from the Sun, from a *kami*, from the ancestors; and we live in this earthly realm. We manifest from Great Nature. We manifest from infinite nature into the relative world." According to Bahá'í teachings, a Michigan educator explains, "the soul emanates from the spiritual worlds and is connected to the body at conception."

From Jewish and Christian perspectives, not only is God the Maker of all that is, there is a sense that each individual is the result of God's intention, that none of us is an accident. For example, the Psalmist says to God, "You yourself created my inmost parts; you knit me together in my mother's womb" (Psalm 139:12). The Islamic point of view is similar. In various verses, the Qur'an says that God has fashioned humanity out of clay, into which God has blown God's spirit. The Qur'an also says that God created humanity created from a single *nafs*—a single self, or soul. "The soul is created by God and enters the womb," says a Shi'ah nurse in Michigan. "Ensoulment takes place around the fourth month of the pregnancy. The body is both a carrying case for the soul, and a gift from God."

Often there is a fine line between explaining where we've come from and explaining what we are. For example, when Mohawk chief Tom Porter talks about personhood, he reminds us that, according to the Haudenosaunee tradition (that is, the nations of the Longhouse Confederacy), humanity was created by Night and Day—the twin offspring of Mother Earth. When we are born, three spirits (or, souls) become braided together like a sweetgrass rope. "So, we come from three sources of energy. Three different sources of energy make us the one person that we are." The first spirit comes from the sky-direction, the realm of the Sky Woman, Grandmother Moon, who gave birth to Mother Earth. The second comes from Mother Earth's energy. "It's like taking coals from a big fire to make a new fire." The third comes from the dirt—Mother Earth's body. That is why Haudenosaunee begin their prayers by taking three big breaths and hollering three times, he says. "It shows the Creator and Mother Earth that we never forgot how we got here."

Hinduism, Jainism, Buddhism, and Sikhism would agree that human beings are caught in *samsara*—the cycle of birth, life, death, and rebirth; a cycle of multiple lifetimes in many forms, from which one hopes eventually to break free. The details of this going around and coming around vary from religion to religion, and sometimes, within a religion. But, ask adherents of these four religions about where we have come from, and the answer will include, "We've been here before"; or, "We've always been." Jains would say that souls are eternal, indestructible, infinite in number, and able to retain their individuality. Whether we call it *atman* or *jiva,* we are referring to something that has always been, and will always be, although it may "seem" to have been born and to die.

Sikhism acknowledges the possibility that we have had previous lives—but, probably not as a human being. "Several things are said about this in the *Guru Granth Sahib,* our scripture," a Michigan educator points out. "One is that human life is really a rare opportunity; human life is difficult to come by. We had to go through many births before we achieved this, so we need to take advantage of it. This may be our only opportunity." Human life is a gift from God, she explains. "The *Guru Granth Sahib* says, 'You've been given this human body, and this is your only opportunity to meet God.' So it is *clear* that human birth is the ultimate birth, because it is the only one that can find God. There are other references saying, 'Don't waste it.' So, the emphasis really is on treasuring the life we have."

We have heard Hindus speak about the *atman*—the self. They might go further, stressing that the *atman* always has been; it never was not. According to the *Bhagavad-Gita*, an engineer in New Orleans's Hindu community points out, the *atman* "is indestructible and eternal; it neither kills nor can it be killed; it is never born, it never dies, and never ceases to be. Weapons cannot pierce it, fire cannot burn it, water cannot moisten it, wind cannot dry it."

But how does the self relate to Ultimate Reality? The *Advaita* school of thought, sometimes called non-dualism or monism, has ancient roots but gained new popularity in the twentieth century when it was embraced by influential people like India's second president. *Advaita* has become quite prominent among American Hindus. Many of them will say that the *atman* emanates from Brahman—that humanity is of the same essence as God. "Think of it this way," says one Detroit mechanical engineer: "If your finger injures your eye, you have a part of yourself hurting yourself. By this same principle, if you hurt the other person, you are hurting yourself—because we are all of the same essence. All consciousness is from the same source," he insists, "and all people are a part of the One God."

But the members of the BAPS temple in nearby Canton see things a bit differently. They are devotees of Swaminarayan (1781–1830 CE), their founding teacher, whom they worship as an *avatar* of Vishnu, thus God himself. "We are *Vishishta Advaita*, qualified non-dualists," their priest explains. As they understand it, while individual *atmans* and things of the material world are real, they are completely dependent on Brahman for their existence and functions. The relationship of self and matter to Brahman is like the relationship of cars on a bridge to the bridge itself—the relationship of what is being supported to what is doing the supporting.

Professor Deepak Sarma represents *Dvaita*, the dualist point of view, the third major Hindu understanding of the divine-human relationship. "In the *Dvaita* world," Professor Sarma explains, "our motto is 'All things are different.' All things are different from one another, and the most difference is between God and the individual self. This is the exact opposite of the *Advaita* position's claim that ultimately, God and the individual self are the same, and that the difference we perceive is an illusion. We say that things exist, and they are different. People are different; selves are different—they are certainly different from God. The individual selves, the deities, and God are in an interesting hierarchy—with God at the top. For the *Advaita,* God is really the same as all material things. In my world, God is totally different. My understanding of God is closer to Christianity in that way."

How might a Buddhist explain where we come from? David Zuniga is a hospital chaplain ordained in the Son (Korean Zen) tradition. "One answer is that our *karma* continues; our action, our deed continues," he says, pointing to the Pali Canon, the most ancient collection of Buddhist texts. Some Buddhists talk in terms of transference of *karmic* energy, a *karmic* seed; they prefer this notion to any thought that an entity or a personality is transplanted somehow from one container to another. "Think of what happens when you light a candle," a Zen graduate student suggests. "It burns down; but just before it exhausts itself, you light another candle from it; and when it burns down, you light another, and so forth. Is the flame on the sixth candle the same as the first one? The answer is 'Yes' *and* 'No.' The essence is passed, but it is technically not the same."

"The continuation of karmic energy is understood in various ways," Reverend Zuniga adds. "Some people think that someone's energy literally continues from life to life. Others see it more metaphorically. For example, the energy of both Martin Luther King and Adolf Hitler continue to affect the world we live in today."

"Another answer we can find in the Pali Canon is that our consciousness continues," he notes. Like *karma,* or karmic energy, "*consciousness* is a bit of a nebulous term and is seen in different ways. Again, the central debate is: How does something continue if we have no selves? Here, the Buddha says that consciousness exists, but it always changes. For example, my consciousness at this precise moment is different from when I first started to answer this question, and it will be different when I am done. So consciousness could continue from life to life, yet still be different. Some schools of Buddhism, especially in Tibetan Buddhism, say that a person's body, speech and mind (or some dimensions of them) continue."

A lay practitioner of Tibetan Buddhism picks up this theme. "Buddhism accepts beginningless lifetimes," he asserts. "That is, since beginningless time, a subtle consciousness has been going from lifetime to lifetime, taking on different bodies based on virtuous or negative actions of body, speech, and mind." That body can manifest as a human, which is considered the best rebirth to have; or, it could manifest in a hell-realm, a realm of suffering. It could also take the form of a 'celestial being.' The celestial realm is a blissful existence, he says, but it is not a good place to land. Since it is so comfortable, one would not desire to escape from *samsara* altogether—which is the goal. From the Tibetan Buddhist point of view, then, the answer to the question of "Where have we come from?" is, "Somehow, we have always existed, though perhaps not in this realm." Pure Land Buddhists would agree.

A key Buddhist principle is the reality of suffering. A second is that the suffering is caused by desire—especially, the desire to prevent things from changing. But, explains the Venerable Piyatissa, the abbot of the New York Buddhist Vihara, change is the very nature of *samsara*. Think of it, he says: "When we came to the room it was nearly 3:30 and now it's nearly 4:30. When we entered this room, we didn't have such knowledge of the *dharma*, of the Buddha's teaching; but now we have enriched our knowledge. Not only that, we are older, stepping forward to death." Only by reducing our craving, anger, and delusion do we come to understand the implication of all this. "We all have the innate ability to do so," he emphasizes, "but we have been misled by many, many births. And we are still wandering."

Where Are We Going?

Whether we speak of *soul* or prefer a word from our religion's home language, all of us know full well that the human *body* is impermanent. Is life in this body all we can expect? Is there a "next stop"? In general, answers from the various religions fall into one of four categories:

- ‿‿ Death is part of a circular (or spiral) process; we live multiple earthly lives, although there is a way out of this cycle.
- ‿‿ After we live this one earthly life, we then go to an "intermediate state"; eventually, we will undergo bodily resurrection, and with that, God's judgment.
- ‿‿ Upon death, we become some sort of non-material being; that is, our soul has "a biography" and it goes on to another special existence in the cosmic realm, but it is never re-embodied.
- ‿‿ We live this one earthly life and that is it; there is nothing more, and any "life" we have after death is in the memory of people who knew us.

"Among Jews, you're going to get all those different answers," a rabbi acknowledges. Indeed, it is the case that a single religion may offer more than one of these answers (or, several variations on the basic answer)—each supported by that religion's sacred texts and traditions. And, since our last answer to "Where have we come from?" was "We have come from a previous life," let's consider notions of reincarnation and rebirth as the first answer to the question of what happens when we die.

Multiple lives
Taoists see death as a continuation of life, but in a new phase, explains a well-known Taoist master in New York. When we die, the *hun* continues; the *p'o* drops away. That is, our intellectual,

moral dimension keeps going, but our earthly part dissipates. The human aspect of the spirit of the deceased stays with the family, he says. To some extent, some aspects of the deceased enter a special realm where a relationship is maintained with the family left behind, "and the heaven-spirit, which is the closest to what the West considers 'soul,' transmigrates."

Mention of transmigration of the soul always brings Hinduism to mind. As a Louisiana engineer puts it, "We Hindus believe that you take birth perhaps as many as 186,000 times." Some Hindus hold to a notion that at the time of cremation, "the *atman* takes off from the skull," a professor explains. "It can choose a path—either the path of light or the path of darkness. If it takes the path of light, then it merges with the flame, and from the flame to the waxing moon, to the light, to the light of lights, and never returns. But, if you had a bad night on the night of cremation, then your *atman* merges with the smoke. That's called the Path of the Fathers. In this mode, the *atman* goes to the rhythm of the waning (rather than the waxing) moon. It goes to darkness, and returns to the earth in a different form. It could be human, it could be animal or plant—whatever."

Samsara, the cycle of birth, death, and rebirth, is driven by *karma*. "What you do in this life will be reflected in your next birth cycle," the engineer continues. "If you do bad deeds, you might take birth as a roach. The human body is the ultimate achievement you can have. If you do really super, you can go away from these life-cycles. You achieve *moksha*, liberation." Practicing *jnana yoga*, *karma yoga*, *bhakti yoga*, or *raja yoga*—the paths of study, selfless service, devotional practices, or disciplines (such as fasting, meditation, and psychological and physical exercises)—will enable us to break out of *samsara* and achieve *moksha*. Our Hindu neighbors differ in what they think happens when *moksha* is achieved, depending on their understanding of how the self relates to Ultimate Reality.

From the *Advaita* perspective, as we have already noted, the *atman* and Brahman are essentially the same. Perceived difference is due to ignorance. When the self sees things as they really are—not as they appear—then *moksha* is achieved, and the self will not remain distinct. "Your *atman* merges with Brahman," says the engineer. "We believe that each person is part of God. You are a fraction of God's creation, so you merge into that entity."

The *Advaita* explanation is very common among American Hindus, but we may hear others. From the *Vishishta Advaita* (qualified non-dualist) point of view, when a self achieves *moksha*, it is in union with Brahman but is not absorbed into it. The self remains distinct but totally dependent, and will spend eternity in service to Brahman. The *Dvaita* position, on the other hand, holds that when the *atman* achieves *moksha*, it is *not* absorbed into Brahman. Rather, God and the self are in union as the eternally distinct Lover and beloved.

In Jain understanding, *karma*, be it good or bad, is residue that clings to the self like iron filings cling to a magnet. The hope is to shed all bad *karmas*, so that *moksha* can be achieved. "In Jainism, once a person dies, his soul immediately leaves the body and reincarnates as something right away," a Jain surgeon explains. "The *karma* you accumulated in this life and previous lives decides what your next life will be," says a pediatrician. "There are four possible destinies: the human realm, the heavenly realm, the animal realm, and hell. When you are dying, the destination of the soul has already been decided. There's another body in preparation. Within a few seconds—almost instantly—the soul has already migrated somewhere else."

This is the case, an obstetrician agrees, "unless the soul has reached purification. That's the ultimate goal of every Jain in this life—to reach that purification of soul. Just like when a mirror is dirty, you want to clean it up. When it is really clean, you can see the pure reflection; that's the state of your soul you want to reach. There are many guidelines for purifying your soul. If one reaches that purification of soul, it doesn't go to another life-cycle."

"Your intention makes a big difference about where you end up in the next birth," a Chicago biochemist explains. As death nears, she says, what is happening in your mind plays a significant role in what happens to your soul next. That is why Jain prayer centers on seeking refuge with the four categories of liberated souls and the desire that one's life may be guided by the principles laid down within them.

"The question of what happens when we die actually gets to the heart of some important debates within Buddhism," a Zen chaplain points out. He reminds us that the Buddha taught the notion of "no self," *anatta*. "Specifically, if nothing exists in a permanent, fixed, distinct way, then what continues from life to life? How do you have rebirth? The Buddha taught on a level that could best be understood by his audience. He didn't teach one thing consistently all the time. That very style of teaching could itself be called *upaya*, skillful means: you help people in a way that is best at their particular point in space and time. So, in the Pali Canon, we find several different answers to the question of what continues. I think the Buddha would say that the correct answer is the one that is most skillful for the particular person—the one that best helps that particular person cope with the Great Matter of birth and death."

Most Buddhists, especially in the American context, avoid the term *reincarnation*. They prefer *rebirth* because it implies that if something continues, exactly *what* lives on is much less fixed. However, some do use the two terms synonymously; and Tibetan Buddhists use both, though they distinguish between them. From the Tibetan perspective, Geshe Sopa explains, rebirth is uncontrolled, due to previous *karma*, previous actions. Reincarnation, on the other hand, is controlled. It is a birth taken on purpose by a Buddha or an *arya-bodhisattva*, someone who has achieved direct insight into ultimate reality in order to be of benefit to others. Thus certain *lamas* are said to have taken reincarnation, while the rest of us have taken rebirth.

From the Tibetan Buddhist point of view, a subtle consciousness has been going from lifetime to lifetime, and will continue to do so. "But it's not like 'John has died, and John is reborn,'" says a lay practitioner. "*John* is just a name put on my body-mind continuum. Subtle consciousness goes on, and in the next life it will be in a different body, and it will have a different label. If you've had a good practice throughout your life, so that you have strong positive states of mind at the death time, that will contribute to a rebirth in one of the three so-called happy states or realms. By the same token, if you have a strong pattern of negative mind, and at the death time you are angry or attached, you'll be propelled into a more profoundly suffering rebirth. It's important to note that there is suffering in the 'happy realms' of cyclic existence. It's just that the pain and discontent isn't as gross and severe as in the lower suffering realms."

"The goal in Buddhism is to escape from that cycle of uncontrolled rebirth," he stresses, "and attain liberation—and ultimately, complete enlightenment, which is the state of a Buddha. Only from the position of full enlightenment can you really help all other living beings in a perfect way. In the Mahayana view, of which Tibetan Buddhism is one expression, we strive toward full enlightenment for the benefit of others. That should be the driving force, the inspiration in everything we do. Uncontrolled rebirth ends after you've become an *arya-bodhisattva*. Then you have *controlled* rebirth. Not only have you attained liberation for yourself, but you have attained a perfect purity by which you can help others."

Pure Land Buddhism, also an expression of Mahayana, gets its name from its teaching about what happens when we die: the notion that somewhere, Amitabha (the Buddha of Boundless Compassion) has prepared a special place for us. This is the Pure Land. Chinese art depicts it as populated by dozens of celestial beings. Amitabha has vowed that whoever believes in the Pure Land, sincerely wants to go there, and calls on him for aid will be transported there. That is, he or she will be released from *samsara*. "They won't come back to this world to suffer any more," a hospital administrator explains.

"If you are practicing the Pure Land tradition and have attained *shin-jin,* which means joyful faith, or awareness of your Buddha-nature, you will be born in the Pure Land—the Enlightenment," says the Reverend T. K. Nakagaki, a Japanese Pure Land priest. The Pure Land may be understood as a stepping stone to Nirvana, but there is also a sense in which the Pure Land and Nirvana are the same," Reverend Nakagaki explains. "Purity is actually freedom from greed, anger, and ignorance. It means you have cleaned your mind and have become free from all those delusions. In a way, the Pure Land is a land that is free from delusions—which means: we are enlightened!" What happens if you are not ready for the Pure Land? "Maybe you will go back to *samsara*," he suggests.

"And of course," a Zen chaplain adds, "some people see the whole teaching of rebirth as a skillful psychological metaphor. For example, if I lose my temper, I am 'reborn' in the hell realm. If I am kind to a patient in the hospital, I am 'reborn' in the heavenly realm. Thus our state of consciousness changes moment to moment in our existence. I tend to be sympathetic to this view."

Regardless, says one Theravada monk, "the teaching is always to do good, be mindful, and prepare your mind. When you do not do anything wrong, your mind is in a pure state, in a way—not totally pure, but at least you will not regret. In the *Dhammapada* it says, 'It is not good to do that kind of action which, later on, you will look back upon with tear-filled eyes.' So it is good and recommended to do any action in a way you can look back upon joyfully. Therefore, as human beings we should always practice loving-kindness, compassion, sympathetic joy, and equanimity. Those are the four sublime states that Buddha encouraged us to develop."

This focus on the here-and-now is important for Sikhs, too, says a Michigan educator. "In Sikhism, we are taught that death is a part of life. We should be preparing for it every day of our life through prayer and meditation, through preparing of our soul." When she works with the young people of her *gurdwara*, her focus is more on the meaning of life and the goal in life, she says, than on what happens when we die. "You're to become free while you're alive, so that while you're alive, your soul becomes one with God. Then the outer covering, your body, won't matter anymore. When you die, your soul will go back to God. If that union doesn't occur, then you will be reborn."

"Sikh scriptures say in several places that the only reason you are born as a human being is so that you can help your soul achieve liberation," says a critical care nurse. "Then the soul can merge into the light of God. They do have a connection—the mind, the body, and the soul. The mind needs to be controlled; and you have to look after the body in order to achieve that state of mind."

"One story has stayed with me," she says. "One of our Gurus loved birds, and when his favorite bird passed away, he said, 'I would also like to have gone and kissed God. Little bird, you are so lucky that you are able to go and kiss God.' When I was younger, I used to say, 'You know, if I die tomorrow, I will get to kiss God, because I am innocent.' It is a wonderful image to teach a child because it removes the fear of death."

"However, we also believe that it is possible to merge with God while one is on this earth itself," she continues. "You merge with God because you have conquered the five sins: greed, anger, attachment, lust, and pride. And also, if you remember God at the end of life, then at the last breath of your life, God is merciful, and you merge into his soul. A couple of our *shabads* (our hymns) say that, in such a case, there is no balancing of the scale. Your account gets torn up. You've already merged."

"The ultimate goal, really, is to become the truth," a professor stresses. In the *Japji,* the Sikh Morning Prayer, Guru Nanak mentions five stages through which the soul must pass. "The first is the realm of the earth, the realm of duty. You reap the benefit of what you do. Here we are on earth, where we are situated between time and space. We are supposed to do our duty, and do the best we possibly can—very much the realization of this world. From here you move on to the second stage: the realm of knowledge. In this realm, we learn and see. From here we go on to the third stage, the realm of beauty. Here your wisdom, your mind, your intellect are sharpened. Then you move on to the realm of rigorous action; then, to the realm of truth."

"These are the five realms," she continues. "But, are they vertical? Are they horizontal?" They might even be concentric circles, with each one bringing the soul nearer to the divine. One thing is clear, however, she stresses: "The Realm of Truth is the ultimate one. You become truth, and then you don't come into this earthly realm—the cycle of birth and death—anymore. You free yourself from that."

"Many Cherokee people believe that you have the potential of seven lifetimes," Dawi Wistona explains. "When you are born the first time, for the sake of illustration, let's say your spirit is this big," he suggests, holding his hands about eighteen inches apart. "Depending on how you live your life, your spirit either grows or shrinks. If you live a good life, a caring life, a life of service, you grow your spirit like you'd grow any muscle. If you live a mean little life, as what my uncle called a 'John-Grabs-All'—that is, you're the kind of person who, when you meet another person, all you can think about is how you can get what you want from him—then you shrink your spirit."

"When you die," Mr. Wistona continues, "your spirit goes to the west for awhile—it's an indeterminate period of time—until you're ready to be born into your next life. You come back with whatever you left with. So if you grew your spirit, that's what you come back with; if you shrunk your spirit, that's what you come back with. The goal is, eventually, to grow your spirit. The example I was given was the metamorphosis of the egg to the caterpillar to the pupa to the butterfly. The idea is that you grow your spirit with each lifetime, and eventually you reach the fullness of your potential."

"When you pass away after that seventh lifetime," he says, "you go to the east, to a place called the Sun Land—a place beyond the sun. I asked my uncle, 'What's it like?,' and he said, 'I don't know. Nobody ever came back and told us!' The way I perceive it is that you actually become a part of the Creation Force at that point, as opposed to being recycled to your component energy."

"On the other hand," Mr. Wistona concludes, "it is also possible to *kill* your spirit. Only you can do that. Only you can grow your spirit; only you can kill your spirit. And if you kill your spirit, it dies, and you're done. You're gone. That's my perception, based on what I've been told, and what I've seen and experienced."

And, perhaps surprisingly, "We live many lifetimes" is a traditionally acceptable Jewish answer to the question of what happens when we die. "Some Jews do believe in reincarnation—in which you get one soul, but its biography traverses many bodies," an Orthodox rabbi acknowledges. "According to this belief, a person's story is going to take generations to work itself out." In fact, by the Middle Ages, reincarnation and transmigration of the soul were quite prominent in some streams of Jewish writing. "Jewish mysticism is heavily into reincarnation," he notes. Do many Jews believe in reincarnation today?

"Judaism is not going to take a head count," he replies. Lots of observant Jews today believe in it. But of course, it's not a required belief."

Bodily resurrection
Christianity's historic creeds affirm "the resurrection of the dead, and the life of the world to come." This means, says Frederick Buechner, that we go to the grave "dead as a door-nail," but that God will give us life back just as we were "given it by God in the first place." In Christian terms, he continues, resurrection means that what God will bring back to life will be "not just some disembodied echo of a human being but a new and revised version of all things which made him the particular human being he was and which he needs something like a body to express." In short, he stresses, from a Christian perspective, life-after-death "is entirely unnatural."[2]

From an Islamic point of view, on the other hand, resurrection is part of the natural order. Muslim spiritual leaders may point, for example, to the rejuvenation of plants every spring-time as affirmation of the certainty of a general resurrection on the Day of Judgment. "We Muslims believe that we go, not 'from life to death,' but from 'life to life,'" a Michigan imam stresses. A number of Qur'an verses make it clear, a Long Island physician points out, that God determines the length of each person's life, that actions have consequences, and that we can choose whether to set our sights on the life-to-come, for which Muslims are encouraged to prepare constantly. "Prophet Muhammad (Peace be upon him) said, 'Work for this life as if we are living forever, and work for the life-to-come as if you are dying tomorrow.'"

"This world is not designed for us to be comfortable in," a Philadelphia hospital chaplain asserts. "This world is designed to teach us things. The next world is the place where, if we manage to get through this world with a degree of honor, we can lay back and enjoy ourselves."

"We are taught that when death comes," a graduate student explains, "the first thing that happens is that an angel comes and asks you three questions: 'Who is your God? What is your religion? What is your Book?' The answer to those questions will come to you, depending on how you lived your life. If you haven't lived your life as a Muslim, then you won't be able to answer as a Muslim."

"We Muslims are taught, and I believe, that the way the soul is extracted from the body depends on our answers to the questions we are asked," says a librarian. "I think there are tests and challenges once we leave this life. And then, we wait! We wait for the Day of Judgment."

"Between the time the person passes away and when the person is raised up again on the Day of Judgment, there's a middle period where we are in the ground," a journalist clarifies. This is the *barzakh*, an intermediate state, which will be comfortable or punishing, depending on the life one led. Muslims sometimes speak of this as the punishment of the grave.

Some Muslims take all of the Qur'anic details about this transition from life to life quite literally, but others do not. "I see them as allegorical illustrations of some sort of preparation for the Day of Judgment," one educator says. "It is in the Qur'an. We accept it as the Word and the Truth of God, but I don't see two angels with their wings and books and pens literally coming and taking notes. I don't see that way. I don't believe there is a sequence of events. The *barzakh* is a timeless, spaceless domain. The Islamic tradition is rich with illustrations and explanations about what happens to people after death, but none of these should be understood as exact explanations of what happens."

Some Muslims are adamant that there is no avenue of communication between souls in the *barzakh* and people who are still living a bodily life on earth. Others feel just as strongly that there is. "When we pass a graveyard," the journalist notes, "we'll say, 'Peace be unto you, People of the Grave,' and we believe they can hear us." A scholar agrees: "We know that the Prophet (Peace be upon him) spoke to people who had been buried; he spoke to them in their graves. And his companions asked, 'Can they hear?' and he said, 'They certainly can hear.' Now tradition tells us that it's not that the soul continues to be *in* the body after death; it continues to be *associated* with the body, and maintains some sort of relationship."

It is worth noting that while American Muslims will often use the terms *heaven* and *hell,* the Qur'anic equivalents are *al-Jannah,* literally, the Garden, but often translated as Paradise, and *al-Nahr,* literally the Fire. The Qur'an does speak of "the heavens." The word is *al-Samawat,* but *al-Samawat* refers to the cosmos; its opposite is *al-Ard,* the Earth. "When the final Day of Judgment comes, there will be a scale to weigh our good and bad deeds," a student explains. On the Day of Judgment, God will decide who shall be admitted to *al-Jannah* and who will be consigned to *al-Nahr.*

What about the promise, often mentioned in the popular press after the September 2001 attacks, that according to Islamic tradition men will be given "virgins in heaven"? Non-Muslims often raise that question these days, sometimes adding, What do the *women* get? "You know, I grew up as a Muslim," says a Detroit resident. "I've also lived in Dubai and in Pakistan. Interestingly, in all the Islamic classes I ever took, this notion of the 'virgins' as reward for martyrdom was never mentioned! The first time I heard about it was when I was president of the Muslim Student Association at my university. After 9/11, the question would come up from time to time. So I started asking imams 'What's the case with this?'"

"It's not in the Qur'an," says one scholar. "Now there *is* a reference to *houris* in the Qur'an. There are beautiful maidens and beautiful youths in the descriptions of Paradise. But this thing about seventy-two virgins for the martyr, maybe it is mentioned in some *Hadiths,* the reports of the Prophet's sayings or deeds. In any case, it's scarcely mainstream." In fact, says another scholar-activist, what the Qur'an does make clear is that, when it comes to devotion to God, humility, chastity, charity, and so on, God's expectations of women and men are the same; and for women and men who meet those expectations, God's promise of forgiveness and reward in the life to come is the same as well.

"The whole concept of the Day of Judgment and the afterlife was taught to us every week when I was growing up, but the one thing we were always told is that God is merciful," a graduate student stresses. "God is just, but he is also very merciful. One of the ways you can see that in the Qur'an is that whenever

God talks about hell, he'll always follow that with a verse about heaven, just to keep you going. Heaven is what you're working towards."

"The Day of Judgment is something that we ponder about a lot," her husband agrees. "For some people it is heaven that drives them to do what they do in life. For some people, it's the fear of hell. For others like myself, it's more the opportunity to be able to see God, and to ask questions that we've had all our lives." "Or," his wife adds, "you worship God because you love him, and you love the religion."

What about Judaism? Judaism speaks of *Olam ha-Ba*, the World to Come. "Remember that, from the time of Rabbinic Judaism onward, resurrection is a key doctrine of Judaism," an Orthodox rabbi stresses. "So, traditional Jews do not question that you 'come back.' I'd say the traditional Jewish answer is, 'We go somewhere. We don't know where exactly. We have a rough name for it. But then, we return.'"

"Then," he continues, "there's the question of, Do you come back forever? Does personhood always require a union of the body and the soul? Most Jewish mystics believe that the answer to that was 'Yes.' In other words, they believe that there is a transformation of the human body at the time of the resurrection, and at that point, the body reveals the presence of God in just the way that the soul does—that the two are in an indissolvable unity. So in the view of the Jewish mystics, body and soul are not natural enemies. They can also be friends. They just need transformation to make that happen."

Special non-material existence
Many religions teach that human beings have body and soul, and that when we die, the soul keeps going. Historically, Zoroastrianism has taught this, Professor K. D. Irani agrees. The union between the soul, the *fravashi* (the divine essence), and the physical body is dissolved at death, he explains. "The *fravashi*, being divine, becomes part of the divinity itself; the soul crosses the Chinvat Bridge, and the body decomposes. But, does the soul maintain individuality, or not? In Zoroastrianism, that is not resolved." In the *Gathas,* the stage of final existence is called "the state of best consciousness," Professor Irani notes.

"Now what exactly do we mean by that? There are people who have felt that this is just 'consciousness,' and that we are no longer an individual. There are others who think there is maintenance of individuality."

Dr. Kersey Antia notes that the Chinvat Bridge, the Bridge of the Separator, "is very specifically mentioned in the *Gathas* by Zarathustra himself. *Chin* means 'choice.' Whatever choice you made comes back to haunt you or reflect you at that time. So, the soul passes over the Chinvat Bridge. If it is a good soul, and the Good Thoughts, Good Words, and Good Deeds outweigh the bad thoughts, bad words, and bad deeds, then the soul passes the bridge; if not, the bridge becomes narrower and narrower, and they slip off into the 'other side.'" And, adds Professor Irani, "If your deeds are roughly equal, you go to a state where you gradually will be purified over many, many years."

Descriptions of the Chinvat Bridge can be quite colorful, with dogs on guard and celestial beings on duty to preside at the soul's tribunal and to help it across. However, says a filmmaker, "I have been taught that the Bridge is metaphorical, and that our soul judges itself. We have created heaven for ourselves here on earth if we have lived a life of Good Thoughts, Good Words, and Good Deeds, and if we've used our minds—which is one of the highest creations of God. If we have lived a thoughtful life, and have created good deeds, if we have been a good person, a respectful person, and a decent person, we pretty much know that our afterlife is also going to be good."

"The point is that our soul keeps evolving," says a young physician. "Our belief is that our physical being is just a vessel for our soul right now on this plane; but in the spiritual plane, our soul is connected to God. Our soul is carrying the deeds we've done. We don't have a heaven and hell *per se*. It's more like, 'Will your soul go back to God, or will it stay in a state of unrest to be judged again at a later time?'"

The Zoroastrian term *frashokereti* sometimes is translated as *resurrection,* but its more literal meaning is *final renovation.* It refers, as Dr. Antia explains, to "a time when, not only all human beings, but also all living creatures will become fresh and pure by the grace of God." Rage, greed, disease, violence, hatred, and all other pollutants will be eradicated. According to the later sacred texts, "all souls, even the evil souls, will be resurrected to a new, perfect life."

Like many of her rabbinical students, one Conservative professor says she doesn't believe in a bodily resurrection. "I believe some piece of us has an eternal component. I believe that some sort of clarification happens in death. Death is one kind of end, but it is not only an end." This is a common viewpoint among Jews, an Orthodox rabbi concurs. He notes that many of today's Jews embrace the teaching of the twelfth-century philosopher Maimonides that "in the end, the body is going to be dispensed with, and we will live eternally in the spirit." But, he says, Judaism definitely has a place for a concept of a unique soul for each body. "There is a fairly standard view that the soul has a biography that goes past the physical body. We all have this one biography with a spiritual component and a physical component. Among Jews there are questions about what the relationship of these two components should or ought to be. Sometimes they are thought to be natural enemies; sometimes they are friends."

Some Jews embrace a notion of an immediate afterlife in addition to the messianic afterlife, an Orthodox educator points out. "Certainly a lot of traditional Jews believe that," she says, "and I think it definitely provides some measure of comfort that there is something eternal. Let's put it this way. The practice of saying the Mourner's *Kaddish* for only eleven months, as opposed to a year, comes from the idea is that someone who has sinned remains in purgatory (or whatever the term is) for a year. And you don't want to say that, God forbid, your parents are in purgatory for a whole year; so you say the Mourner's *Kaddish* for just eleven months."

"Something happens to the soul after the body dies," an Orthodox rabbi insists. "It could be that it goes to some very special place. Even in the *Tanakh,* and certainly by the time of Rabbinic Judaism, you find that notion of a place called *Sheol.*" Indeed, a Michigan rabbi notes, "during the thousands of years of our tradition, you will find belief in the reality of a heaven and hell. However, some Jews believe only in a good place to which we all go."

"My personal belief has evolved over time," admits a Michigan hospital chaplain. "I remember as a child being taught that we Jews only believe in heaven; there's no hell. But in looking at this world and everything we see, I have come to my own understanding that there is some reward and punishment beyond this world. That's how I make sense of the things that go on around me. Now, I may be wrong, but I am comfortable in saying that is how I feel right now—that reward and punishment may come in the next life."

"Where do people go when they die? They don't *go* anywhere," a Bahá'í business consultant asserts. "They are very close by. You may not see them, but they are here. Bahá'u'lláh speaks of the next world as an entirely spiritual experience. He says it is as different from this world as this world is different from the world of the womb."

"We Bahá'ís believe we can continue to progress in the next world based on the virtues we acquire in this world," a New York businesswoman explains, "and based also on the prayers from this world, and the mercy of God." A physical body will be unnecessary, a consultant agrees, "but some of our internal senses will be needed very much."

"There are lots of writings on these other worlds of God," notes Professor Paula Drewek, a lifelong member of the Bahá'í Faith. "They are understood to be unlimited, and spiritual. We have no teachings at all about an eventual physical resurrection of the body, since the worlds beyond this one are without time and space. Since we have the condition now of the physical body, we really can't envision those worlds. But the Bahá'í writings tell us they are unspeakably glorious—that our eyes will be opened, that our understanding of truth will be clarified. We will rejoice with the souls who have devoted themselves in their love for God. We will rejoice in circling round the reality of God in the next world. It sounds to me like a wonderful condition that I guess I am looking more forward to, now that I am getting older."

"Bahá'u'lláh says, 'I have made death a messenger of joy to thee. Wherefore dost thou grieve? I have made the light to shed on thee its splendor. Why dost thou veil thyself there from?' If we think of it in that context," Paula explains, "what veils us from the splendor of God is really our own ignorance. We have the ability to turn ourselves toward God, to be enkindled with the love of God, and with knowledge of God, and with faith in God. That describes our purpose, so that when death hits—and it *is* a joyful occasion—we return to the source of our being; we return to that spiritual kingdom for which we are created."

Shinto is joyful and very life-oriented, yet it does address the question of what happens when people die. "Basically, when we die, there's a parting of the road," a priest explains. "The physical body and the *mitama*, the soul, separate. The *mitama*, over a period of fifty days, becomes spiritualized—or raises in vibration—and returns to the *kami*-realm. They become *soreisya*— that is, ancestral deities, different from *kami*."

The religions of America's First Nations each have their own perspective on what happens when we die. As the Ojibway see it, a nurse explains, "We come from the east when we are born into the world. When it is time to leave, we leave through the Western Doorway. If you look at the constellations, there are times when the Milky Way has a path through it. It is during that time, during the change between night and morning, that the Great White Horse will come to carry out a loved one and take him home."

"The traditional Cherokee belief," says healer Dawi Wistona, "is that when we die, our spirits go to the west to what is called the *Usvhiyi*, the Darkening Land. You live a shadow-life in the Darkening Land, doing what you did here."

"For the first year after death, we believe that the spirit wanders, and says goodbyes," notes Keetoowah author Yvonne Wakim Dennis. "And that's why, when a person dies, we do not speak his or her name for the first year. You don't want to call the spirit; that's rude. It would be like clicking your fingers to a waiter. So you wait for the person to visit. It's happened to me. I would notice little, subtle things. I wouldn't realize that's what it was until afterwards."

The traditional Keetoowah belief is that after that first year, one "goes home" to the Spirit World. "What I personally believe," she concludes, "is that, as a human, I don't have the right to fantasize about the afterlife; I have to wait. I believe in experiential learning. So it is not for me to sit here and say,

'When I die, this is what will happen.' That would be arrogant. I'm just a mortal being. It's not for me to know certain things. What happens after death is a great mystery to me, but ritualizing the difficult times in life consoles us and gives us a reason to keep living."

"In Vodou, there is the notion that we make a contract with God," explains Dowoti Désir, who is both a priest and a scholar of Afro-Atlantic traditional religion. "We make a contract with God before we're born that we are going to be this particular kind of person, and we are going to do particular things." In Vodou, there is also the notion that each of us is "the summation of the will and the spirit of those who came before us," she continues. By becoming the summation of many things, "we become what we call in Vodou a *pwen*—a point, literally; a star in the sky. Our spirit, our soul, our person becomes a star."

"In Afro-Atlantic traditions, there is a sense that when we die, the physical body is done, but the *gwo-bon-zanj*, the spirit or soul, continues to inhabit the world for a time," she continues. "There is a period of about ten days between one's physical death and one's transition to the realm of the ancestors. We are hovering here."

"I had a funny conversation with my cousins the other day," says Professor Désir. "We were on our way to a baby shower, and we realized it was the fifteenth anniversary of our grandmother's death. I asked, 'Have either of you ever seen or spoken to her since? What were your experiences like?' One cousin told me she had seen her in a mirror. Another cousin talked about how our grandmother would come visit her in her dreams. I have had a similar experience. With almost every member of my family who has passed, always about ten days later, they come to me. It's clear that they have made their transition. They let me know, 'This is where I am; this is the place I am in.' Most of them were in an okay place. They were at peace. We did not need to be concerned."

"One of the things my cousin shared with me is that our grandmother was buried without her shoes on! Why? Because her daughters felt, 'We don't want her coming back to visit us.' So there is clearly this distinct impression that even though the physical body can disintegrate, a physical presence is still very much capable of making itself manifest in our world. Instead of joining the world of the invisibles, the mysteries, the dead are physically with us, and we are conscious of the fact that they are here. So, my cousins removed our grandmother's shoes and buried her with her shoes off—to slow her down a bit!"

Nothing more
Traditionally, the Mohawk understanding of what happens when we die has not included the concept of heaven and hell, a chief stresses. That notion comes with a "fear component," and for Mohawks, "that's a completely foreign concept." What you've done during your life has no bearing on what happens when you die, he explains. From a Mohawk perspective, a human has three souls, three spirits. "It's like a braid. The three become one while we live on this earth. When we die, those three spirits unravel and go back to their original places. Two return to the Earth, and the third one goes back to the Sky."

When we die, "we go to the cemetery—period," declares one English teacher, himself an observant Jew. For some Jews, the notion of *pikuach nefesh,* preservation of life, leads to an emphasis on life in this world over any sense that there will be life in another world to come. Some would assert that "the only thing that lives on is memory: we return to the earth, just as God created us from this earth," one rabbi says.

Similarly, some Buddhists—particularly Zen practitioners—are not sure that *anything* truly continues when we die. "This position is often described as 'full stop,'" says a Zen chaplain. Again, he reminds us, "the Buddha gave various answers to the question of what happens when we die," and this answer is also found in the Pali Canon. "The Buddha taught we are all collections of elements, such as our minds, our bodies, and such. When we die, everything just ends."

"There is this Buddhist notion that we see within in a very limited frame with this body," explains a chaplain at a Houston cancer center. "Death is a transition or a doorway into the complete realization—if one does not have it in one's lifetime—that there isn't a 'me.' I am part of this whole stream that is 'birthing and deathing' and 'birthing and deathing.' We already have Buddha-nature; it is already within us. We haven't yet awakened to the fact that it's already there. This process of birth and death is what we do in our lifetime to wake up to this."

"One of my fellow monks told me this beautiful story of when he was in India," recalls chaplain David Zuniga. "One night, as he was sitting on the bank of the Ganges, meditating and watching the many, many funeral pyres around him, he wondered, 'What happens to people when they die?' Then a thought came to him, 'I don't know.' And as he told me that story, he had the most beautiful smile on his face. He said, 'David, I have no idea what happens to us when we die.' That's kind of a good story to illustrate a Zen approach."

"In Buddhism, we would say that all beings are radically interconnected," Reverend Zuniga reminds us. "Nothing exists in a discrete, individual, autonomous, distinct way. In Buddhism, there is no self, there is no other; there is just pure existence. Death is certainly a change, but existence itself is what always continues."

"Here's the problem," says Sevan Ross, a priest who serves Chicago's Zen community. "When you talk about any kind of personality or solidness lasting from one container to the next container, you are now running completely counter to what the Buddha taught. What the Buddha taught was that there is no container; that all of this is one moving verb. We are *change*. We are not *changing;* we are *change*. There is nothing you can lay your hands on and say, this is solid. So when you talk about a personage passing from this lifetime to the next lifetime, it is hard to synchronize that with the Buddha's teaching of *anatman*—'no self.'" Indeed, he exclaims, "What 'self' would it be that continues? To talk about where 'I' go when 'I' die is a difficult question is Buddhism, because 'I' am always here! Whether I'm dead or not, I'm always here; there's nowhere to go!"

Being Human

"We debate and discuss," one rabbi says, "but what we believe— we have a lot of leeway in terms of opinion." She could be speaking of many of her neighbors, whatever their religion. And so it is with the questions Gauguin painted. One religion's texts and teachings may support several answers, especially when it comes to the question of "Where are we going?"

"I urge my colleagues to get in touch with what they think about this question," says a Michigan rheumatologist, herself a devout Hindu. "We physicians deal with life and death every day. We must get a grip on our own understanding of what will happen when we ourselves die."

At the Massachusetts College of Pharmacy and Health Sciences, Professor Rick Shifley offers an elective course on death and dying. For one assignment, he explains, "the students are supposed to write about end-of-life care; they are literally to write about what they themselves want after they die." In the past, he says, his students typically would write out of the faith tradition in which they were raised. Recently, more and more of them seem to have had little or no exposure to a specific tradition; most are exceedingly illiterate when it comes to religion. He tries to help his students appreciate how essential it is for health professionals to know how to talk with and listen to the dying and their families with some appreciation of their beliefs and customs. He tells them about a woman who grew up in Boston's heavily Catholic South End, but whose first job after nursing school was at a hospital in Hawai'i. "People were ill and were dying. In the South End of Boston, she would have just called a Catholic priest, but in Hawai'i it was different. Her patients practiced religions from Japan; they practiced religions from Taiwan; they practiced the native Hawaiian religion. It was a big adjustment for her. I am trying to get my students to look at some of these things, because they too will have to adjust."

Regarding the question of where we've come from, the line between the answer to this question and the others is sometimes rather blurred. When it comes to the question of "What are we?," we all agree we are a body with something else, but we vary in our name of that something and in our descriptions of its relationship to the physical body. And while we differ on the details, we all agree that we are *persons*. At the very least, says one Christian physicist and theologian, that makes us "a self-conscious being, able to use the future tense in anticipation, hope, and dread; able to perceive meaning and to assign value; able to respond to beauty and to the call of moral duty; able to love other persons, even to the point of self-sacrifice."[3] We are mortal—at least physically; we inhabit bodies that have breakdowns; and illness raises its own variety of issues in multireligious America. It is to these concerns that we now turn.

Notes

1. Frederick Buechner, *Wishful Thinking: A Theological ABC* (New York: Harper and Row, 1973), 41.
2. Buechner, *Wishful Thinking*, 42–43.
3. John Polkinghorne, *Faith, Science, and Understanding* (New Haven: Yale University Press, 2000), 11.

CHAPTER TWO

When We're Ailing

"WHEN I WAS LIVING in Atlanta a few years ago," recalls a graduate student, "a hospital chaplain asked me to come and give a little lesson on how to manage pastoral care for terminally ill Hindu patients and their families. As a Hindu myself, I appreciated his desire to know." In this chapter, we will listen to how the religions of some of our neighbors help them understand health and illness, what they wish the nurse or doctor or hospital chaplain would understand about them as persons of faith, and some thoughts from chaplains and medical personnel on the intersection of health, illness, and religion.

Attitudes Toward Illness

Sitting with suffering
"It has been said that of all the world's religions, Buddhism focuses most directly on suffering and death. I think that's

true," says the Reverend David Zuniga. Buddhism says that suffering is the teacher. As a chaplain, Reverend Zuniga has had particular experience in cancer care. When confronted with suffering, his Buddhist sensibilities keep him from trying to alter it. However, he says, "We can transform our own reaction to the event. For example, a person might have a terminal form of cancer. In this case they cannot alter the reality of their cancer; they are going to die. But by sitting with it, by being fully present to it and learning from it, by applying the teachings of Buddhism and directly facing the totality of the experience, they can then cultivate equanimity and joy amidst their terminal illness. Although they may not alter the physical reality, in this way they can spiritually transform their reality."

"The difference between altering and transforming may be subtle," Reverend Zuniga continues, "but it is quite important. This also illuminates the difference between pain and suffering. Everyone feels various forms of pain sometimes. To live is to experience pain. But suffering is being stuck, being caught in cyclical states of spiritual delusion. A person with terminal cancer might experience great physical pain. But at the same time, they can do spiritual practice in a way that liberates them from their suffering. In this way, our great difficulties become great spiritual teachers and even great spiritual gifts."

"The Buddha did not say what causes illness," explains a Theravada monk on Staten Island. "He said: 'This is inevitable, the four fears that come to us: birth, old age, disease, and death. Always, you have to expect these four.' This is said many places in the ancient texts."

"Before he became the Buddha," a Zen practitioner in Michigan clarifies, "Siddhartha Gautama was the son of a king, and he lived a very lavish life. The king wanted his son to become his successor, so he tried to isolate him from the real world. However, Siddhartha's teacher arranged for the young man to encounter the Four Passing Sights: he saw a sick person; he saw an aged person; he saw a dead body being carried to cremations; and he saw a happy, wandering mendicant. Siddhartha asked, 'What's wrong with that person?' And his teacher said, 'That person is ill. Yes, you will become ill. Yes, you will become old. Yes, you will die. And that person's happy because he has given up everything. He's wandering in very simple clothes, just looking for the truth.' It was the fourth revelation that prompted him to leave his father's castle and go out into the jungle, the forest, and seek the truth. So, illness is really a part of the process of life, just as aging and death is."

Whereas Buddhism teaches about sitting with suffering, the Torah supports the notion that there should be medical specialists who alleviate suffering and help people heal. The Talmud teaches the Jewish people that they must live in a community that includes a physician. Thus, many Jews would say, it is God's wish that healthcare be available, offered, and received.

"Why do bad things happen to good people? You're going to find multiple Jewish answers," says Rabbi Tzvi Blanchard. "One answer would be: We don't know. It hasn't been given to us to really understand, either in general or in detail. That's not a terribly satisfying answer for many people, but there are Jews who believe that. All the way on the other end is that if we are perceptive enough and know the situation well enough, we can say exactly why bad things happen."

"Now the middle view is more interesting to me," Rabbi Blanchard says. "We're not prophetic; therefore we can't know the details, but we have to believe that the universe is not a moral crapshoot; and there is some way of coming to understand it. But, because we don't see enough of the world, enough of reality, we are not able to know. Sometimes we think we can know. We'll say, 'Why is it that they haven't found cures for diseases for good people yet? Those good people are suffering because more money hasn't been spent attempting to fix what they've got.' The response is that some of it is due to human beings and some of it is due to the inherent imperfections of a material universe. By the Rabbinic period, we're hearing, 'We don't know why the righteous suffer and the bad prosper.' We don't know, but since we have to adopt *some* position, we say that the universe is hospitable to moral striving—that there's a coincidence of good fortune and good behavior in principle."

"And there's also the position that we can explain the suffering that's due to us and we can figure out how to fix it, but we don't know what caused it. For example, the view in the Talmud is that you can't say that you fell ill because you did something wrong. But, if you fall ill, that's the time for you to examine your deeds to see if there's something that needs correction. It's a sophisticated position, because it depends what you're asking. Do you want God's answer to the question? You're not going to get that! That's what the Book of Job is about. But if you want a human answer to the question, then you're going to have to make do with the evidence that's available to human beings. So, some people say: We do know well enough in a number of cases that we are actually at fault for certain evils. We should focus on those. When bad things befall us, we should focus on what we could have done so that the world would have turned out better."

For help in understanding illness and suffering, Imam Yusuf Hasan explains, Muslims consult the Qur'an. "God says he will only give us good. Whatever bad comes, comes from man's own hand. If we're sick and have cancer or some disease, we don't ask God, 'Why did you put this on me?' If we knew the answer, then we would be the gods! The point is that when we ask 'Why?' we are showing that we don't understand that there is another force at work, the force of evil, trying to make us lose faith in God. It can only attack our physical bodies. It can give us pain and hardship. But it cannot really touch this human being that's inside of me—my soul, my goodness, my righteousness. That is what God says he created in us: this faith and trust in him. He's still in charge, and we can't lose this little amount of faith that we have, even if it's the amount of a mustard seed. In the end, the believer will be victorious. This is the understanding of the Muslim."

If God is in charge, then (one might ask) why take medication? Why not just trust in God for healing? The Islamic Medical Association of North America reminds Muslims that the Prophet himself took medicine when he was ill, and advised his followers to do likewise. While Muslims are to face illness patiently and prayerfully, God wants suffering to be alleviated, and Muslims are required to search for a remedy.

What goes around comes around
"From what I know," says a Hindu physician in the eastern United States, "your *karma* will influence what kind of body

you will get in the next life, what kind of diseases you will be subject to. As you sow, so you shall reap. The way you live is going to determine what you will be in your next life." Adherents of religions that see life as a *karmic* spiral may see a relationship between diseases and accidents and behaviors in past lives.

"On some level," says a Michigan Sikh educator, "these things happen because of our actions, thoughts, and deeds. Everything has a repercussion. That is the answer to why we take birth in certain forms. It always made sense—why some people take birth in a particular environment that I guess you would call 'good,' or another environment that is like a living hell." However, she emphasizes, "*bad* and *good* are human constructs." When illnesses and accidents strike, Sikhs try to keep this in mind. "Really, ultimately, we would say, nothing is bad that is created by God—and *everything* is created by God. We don't have the full picture."

"We as human beings do experience pain," she stresses. "Part of that is our own fault. The human vices of anger, attachment, greed, pride have made this web of *maya*—this web of illusion, that tells us what's good and what's bad in our own human construct. When we get to the point where we are one with God, then we will have the vision that God has—and we'll realize that it is all part of the game. Everything that takes birth will die; everything that comes will go; and all the things that we are experiencing in our life are not the real thing we're after. It's illusion; it's a game, and really what we're after is finding our true self, our true home, which is God, which is inside of us. From a Sikh viewpoint, it's not just the body that we have to treat, but the mind, the spirit as well. Our scripture says, 'The cure of all illnesses is in God's Name.'"

"The theory for many Hindus, Buddhists, and Sikhs is that you are attracting the good and bad *karma*," says a Jain internist. "The idea is that you should avoid attracting the bad *karma*. But Jainism teaches that you should not have *any* kind of *karma*. And that's why, no matter what kind of *karma* it is, once it has attached to your soul, then it is not pure soul."

"*Karma* does not decide what disease you are going to get," a Jain obstetrician insists. "But, Jainism advocates a healthy lifestyle: eat well, drink well, think properly—try always to have the positive thoughts. With a healthy lifestyle, your body has strong enough immunity."

"And when you are sick," says a Jain family physician, "Jainism teaches how to take that sickness. If you work with illness positively, you heal faster."

Closely related to notions regarding present misfortune and misdeeds in past lives is the belief that illnesses stem from sins in the present life. A Bahá'í businesswoman in Michigan points to a passage in the writings of 'Abdul'l-Bahá, the son of Bahá'u'lláh (the faith's founder), which reads: "It is certainly the case that sins are a potent cause of physical ailments. If humankind were free from the defilement of sin and waywardness...it is undeniable that diseases would no longer take the ascendant, nor diversify with such intensity." So, members of the Bahá'í Faith may see illness as an opportunity to atone for past sinfulness.

It's about balance
"In the Bahá'í Faith," says Professor Paula Drewek, "we see the human being as both spiritual and material. Bahá'u'lláh tells us that these two are interrelated. So, if you are treating one aspect, you need to treat the other as well. When healthcare professionals address you as though you were more than just a 'body' with body parts, that you also have spirit, it changes the whole attitude of healthcare toward the individual who is being served. Bahá'u'lláh says that if you have physical ailments, you are to turn to competent doctors and physicians. But there is also the possibility of spiritual causes for illness. In that case, you need a spiritual cure. An individual with a strong faith has a center for his or her life. That center needs to be addressed when you are addressing the individual's health."

One Keetoowah teacher agrees heartily. "We believe that illness is fourfold: physical, spiritual, emotional, and mental," she explains. "All four aspects have to be in balance to heal. A healing is quite an event. It can be very, very exhausting for the person healing you. It requires a lifestyle change; it's not just taking something and feeling better."

From a Taoist perspective, all things possess *qi,* which can be translated as "energy." Sat Chuen Hon teaches *Qigong*—methods for working with the energy of the major organs (heart, lungs, liver, spleen, kidneys). When *qi* flows freely between the organs (and between all parts of the body, for that matter), he explains, we have health; when *qi* is blocked or stagnant, we have sickness.

A Won Buddhist minister nods. "The body complains because it has lost the balance," she asserts. "It is critical in modern life to have a balance: balance between outer world and inner world; balance between your work and your leisure or contemplation or meditation; balance between active engagement and silence; balance taking place in your body, mind, too."

This minister has had to deal with a persistent debilitating illness of her own. During that ordeal, she says, "the question of the human body and the nature of the human condition was critical to contemplate! Won Buddhist scripture speaks about integration of body and mind. It teaches that we must take care of our body and our mind equally. Sometimes, as religious persons, we tend to put more emphasis on mind and spirit than on our body. But it was my painful recognition that I had not followed our teaching. I was putting too much attention on my mind and spirit, and was neglecting my body. Imbalance took place. If you break the balance, then illness comes into your body. It demands that you come back to the center."

How does one meet that demand? "In Won Buddhist meditation, we practice breathing to our 'lower dungeon,'" she explains. "We talk about three centers in the body: upper center, dealing with intellect, wisdom; middle center, dealing with your compassionate feeling, your emotion; and third center, three finger widths below your navel, is your lower dungeon. This is the center of serenity. In Won Buddhism, you are cultivating your lower center."

"Our scriptures tell about the six essentials," she continues. "The three essentials for your mind are wisdom, compassion, and serenity; the three for your body are food, shelter, and clothing. So nutrition is critical for your body and your mind. Exercise is critical. Rest for body and mind is critical—and meditation is a form of rest. During my illness, I meditated a lot. Through meditation, you feel the energy shifting in your body; balance is taking place in your mind and body at the same time."

"If your spirit becomes tired, you'll get sick," a Shinto priest stresses. "For Shinto-followers, purification is about purifying your soul—to make your soul, your spirit more alive. Then you feel fine. Keeping your spirit healthy is very important. Keeping your spirit healthy will keep you body healthy." This is why, she says, Shinto has little to say about the cause of illness. Rather, Shinto places most of its emphasis on being pure to face the day in good fashion.

So does Mohawk spirituality. "We never complain," says a Mohawk spiritual leader; for Mohawks, "not complaining" is a primary healthcare practice! "Illness comes because you don't have peace in your mind. When you have negative things in your mind, and you're always worrying, you're always gossiping about somebody, or you don't tell the truth about things, you're not honest, then that makes an intensity in your body, in your system. It turns into heart trouble; it turns into cancer. It manifests itself. It's like a boil. When you've got something wrong with your system, the pus comes out! It's a simplistic way of looking at it, but it's probably true."

"Traditional" versus "Western"

Taking one's religion seriously means, for some Americans, taking seriously the healing methods associated with that religion's traditional culture—such as the *Ayurvedic* techniques of India, Chinese acupuncture, or Native American and Afro-Atlantic herbal treatments and ceremonies. But what will be the relationship between "traditional" and "Western" medicine for the person of deep religious conviction?

"In my family this drama plays out," Sat Chuen Hon remarks. He is trained in classical Chinese medicine, while his two brothers have studied Western medicine and pharmacology. "It is very interesting when we get together. There is no fight between the two approaches; just personal choice. From my perspective, we should integrate the two. This is my mantra: Western diagnostic is supreme; Chinese treatment is superior. Think about that. Western diagnostic is very concrete, but the treatment is lacking. Basically, it is painkiller, antibiotic, or surgery. All of those have terrible side effects. But Chinese treatment of meditation, herbology, acupuncture, chanting, or music has no side effects (or very few). I say to my students: energy matters in most medical treatments. Medical treatment is not effective if it poisons you. That goes with the classical Hippocratic oath: 'At least, do no harm.' I think Chinese traditional medicine really follows that spirit." Therefore, he stresses, "if you have acute appendicitis, then get surgery! If you have a bad infection, then take antibiotics. But with chronic sickness, Chinese treatments are wonderful!"

"Native People recognize that there are a lot of new diseases that we don't know about," a Mohawk leader stresses. Even our Medicine Ladies and Medicine Men can tell when we have something that won't get better with traditional medicine. They'll say, 'If you go to the doctor, you'll find out for sure.' We want to work together."

The hospital emergency room is great for repair after an accident, says a Keetoowah writer, but Western physicians have not been very successful in managing her chronic illnesses. "So, two months ago, I went to a Cherokee medicine man—a very kind man, one of the best herbalists in the country. I asked him to do a healing. I did what I was supposed to: I took him presents. I really don't want to talk about what he used, because I don't have permission, but I can say that he worked with certain sacred objects. There's no charge for this. I have to pay for the medicine, of course, but there's no charge for his doctoring. That's how you can tell when someone is a real, true healer."

Access to affordable Western-style medical care is a big problem for many people. American Indian Health and Family Services of Southeast Michigan (AIHFS) is one of several dozen urban Indian healthcare centers around the United States that try to bridge this gap. Like most of them, AIHFS has a full medical team that includes a psychologist and a psychiatrist. The center is unusual, however, in that the healthcare it provides is "spirit-based," says Lucy Harrison, who served AIHFS as executive director for many years. Her own training in public health nursing was amplified with simultaneous study of traditional Ojibway ways.

With the barest of resources AIHFS provides substance abuse treatment, various screening clinics, after-school and summer programs for children, and palliative care—all in the context of the spirituality of the Three Fires Nation: the Ojibway (often spelled Ojibwe), Potawatomi, and Odawa peoples. For this reason, the center has earned the name *Midewin*. Sometimes translated as Medicine Society, *Midewin* traditionally refers to the community of authorized healers. "In my Ojibway language," Ms. Harrison explains, "*Midewin* means 'the good life'—and a whole lot more than that, which is tied in with prayer. It serves as the philosophy for our policies. Everything that we do, we do with prayer."

"Traditional Medicine is really about spirit," she asserts. "We cannot do the work without speaking about the spirit, without prayers, without celebration of life, without welcome to the four directions. That's primary. When people come here to get healing, it's mental, physical, and spiritual. They want help. It's okay if they want to ask the nurse or the doctor to smudge or to have a prayer with them; or to 'sweat lodge.' Some people will take the Western medicine and smudge it down and bless it. It's total, complete healing. We are fortunate that we can still hold old ceremonies right here. As we travel through life and deliver healthcare, it is very important that we maintain our spiritual health. Keeping all of our old ceremonies, keeping all of our teachings alive, is the way we keep our responsibilities up."

"I'm very privileged that I've been chosen to work with the elders," she continues. "We have elders who come to our center every month to conduct ceremonies from birth through the end of life; and sometimes we get called into hospitals to do our work. We help our people get ready for the exchange of the physical world, for the end of life, in the Indian way. There's no greater honor than to do the work that will bring them full circle."

AIHFS grows much of what it uses for traditional treatments. "The idea behind our healing gardens was to bring back a number of the perennial medicines that once were plentiful in this region. We also grow our own tobacco in our tobacco garden. Tobacco is very important. We carry it and use it on a daily basis." AIHFS uses tobacco ceremonially, but it also works strenuously against substance abuse of all kinds (tobacco included). "Everything on this earth is given to us for the medicine," Ms. Harrison emphasizes. "That's how they're taking it from a spiritual connotation: don't abuse that medicine!"

Knowing what to use, and using it with care, is equally important among practitioners of the Afro-Atlantic religions, such as Vodou. *Manbo* and *houngan* are Congo terms for women and men with the authority to be "Keeper of the Medicinal Packet"—thus, having the ability to heal. They use leaves, roots, and herbs to treat moral and physical maladies, a Vodou *manbo* explains. "The Vodou temple itself is a site where much treatment actually takes place; and acts of healing are really based on a knowledge of botany. There is a heavy emphasis on that. One really has to know medicinal leaves, roots, and herbs for treating people. And for many of the kinds of illnesses, that works. But I can't say that if one has cancer, these indigenous medical practices and this traditional knowledge will be able to assist a patient. So there's another level of medical knowledge and training that Vodou priests and our community as a whole have to learn. We have to understand that we can take things but so far." On the other hand, she stresses, when Western-style healthcare professionals dismiss traditional religious healing practices as "mere superstition," this can actually keep people who trust these methods from being willing to accept the Western-style medical treatment they need.

In fact, we may know physicians whose initial training was "Western-style" or "conventional," but who now incorporate other methods into their practice of medicine. "I was taught none of that in medical school," says Dr. Jill Baron, a family physician who practices integrative medicine. "But I teach about this now. We need the modern technology, but we need so much more healing. The mind-body connection is so powerful. Loss can compromise our immune system. So, when I see patients in my practice, in my initial history questionnaire I ask them about things like whether they are happy, and what their lives were like when they grew up. It gives me insight. I do all the Western things to get my diagnosis; then I approach the patient in a mind-body kind of way."

Patient Preferences

As each of these adherents of traditional healing has indicated, sometimes the hospital is indeed the best place to deal with what ails us. As America has become more visibly religiously diverse, healthcare professionals have become more aware of the ways in which religious customs and sensibilities affect medical treatment. As a result, some hospitals have developed guidebooks to patient preferences. Similarly, several small handbooks for hospital chaplains outline the basics of various religions. These are helpful, but they have their limits.

Some hospital guides to patient preferences use ethnic categories—but a single ethnicity may include several religions. For example, Americans from the Indian subcontinent may indeed be Hindu, but many are Sikh or Buddhist, Muslim or Jain, Zoroastrian or Christian. And, within any one religion, we may find ethnic variations on belief and practice.

"Hospital protocols on patient preferences are thoughtful, but they also tend to stereotype," says a Hindu student at Harvard Divinity School. Too often they describe what it means to be an adherent of these religions in terms of highly observant practice. "In an attempt to be extra sensitive, they get too obsessive about certain details."

"People want a checklist," says a transcultural nurse, herself a Shi'ah Muslim. "They want to be able to say, 'Oh, you're a Muslim patient. That means you'll want this, this, and this.' It is far more complex than that! Not everybody fits the bill." As we look at a few categories of religion-based patient preferences, we will try to get a sense of the range in each. We'll begin with an overriding concern for many devout people: what the hospital provides at mealtime.

Hospital food

One theme emerges from almost every conversation about what our devout neighbors wish their healthcare providers understood about them while they are hospitalized: religiously mandated diet. This goes beyond complaints about hospital food because it isn't "home cooking." It is not quite the same as the notion of "comfort food"—eating or drinking something we associate (perhaps from childhood) with making us feel better. It has everything to do with the fact that being made to violate our religion's food rules will make us feel worse than our ailment is making us feel already. As one Conservative rabbi puts it, "Giving non-kosher broth to your patient in the cardiac unit is not going to help his heart condition!"

"I would be sure to ask your Buddhist patients whether they'd prefer a vegetarian meal," a Zen leader in Michigan suggests. "Being a vegetarian is nothing a Buddhist is absolutely bound to. The Buddha ate meat. But many Buddhists today are vegetarian, because of the way animals are ill-treated and slaughtered inhumanely."

"If I had to be hospitalized," says a professor, "I'd be sure the staff knew I'm a Hindu. One reason is to make sure I got vegetarian food. When one is ill or injured, one does not want to have to wonder, Are there animal products in this meal?—not to mention that by Indian standards, hospital food is especially bland." Hindus follow a range of dietary practices. Many Hindus are strict vegetarians. Those who do eat meat usually avoid beef and beef products—which would include gelatin salads and desserts. Some avoid onions and garlic. Some avoid eggs; others eat them. Some use dairy products, but not cheese. ("Cheese is rotten milk!" declares one Hindu chaplain.) For others, cheese is fine.

Because of the seriousness with which they take the principle of *ahimsa* (non-harming), an internist explains, strict Jains avoid eating after sunset in order to avoid consuming a tiny insect inadvertently. They avoid root vegetables (since harvesting them will disturb small living beings that live below ground), or multiseeded plants (such as broccoli, eggplant, tomatoes, raspberries, guava)—since each seed is a potential living being and also may be home to worms or hard-to-see insects. Jains prefer to drink water that has been boiled or filtered water to be sure microscopic life has been removed from it. Eggs are considered "living," so Jains may prefer to avoid breads and sweets made with eggs. However, some Jains do use milk products, and may even consume yogurt—even though it is fermented (thus, "living"). "You have to eat some living thing to survive," stresses a family physician. "Jainism categorizes organisms according to the number of senses they have. You try to go to those with the lowest number of senses when you must kill to survive."

Again because of their practice of *ahimsa* (non-harming) and strict vegetarianism, some Jains may be uncomfortable having things made of leather, silk, and fur in their hospital room. They may bring vegetarian concerns to which medications they receive, an internist observes. "Some medications are in gelatin capsules, which Jains may not want to take. I try to avoid all medications containing animal products, and I try my very best to see that my family does not take them, or at least that they know that animal products are involved."

"It is a question of how to be vegan yet be treated in the modern medical world," says a pediatrician. "Jainism teaches that eating or killing any animal creates *himsa;* it creates harm. If you go to the extreme you cannot take polio vaccine, or so many other things. But, if you become paralyzed, what *himsa* would you be creating for your family? So, you think about it and come up with some solution."

"Having kosher food available for your Jewish patient—that's big!" emphasizes a Jewish hospital chaplain. Keeping kosher means sticking to meat from animals and birds that have been slaughtered and preserved according to specific guidelines. It means not eating meat and dairy in the same meal, and waiting a specified length of time after eating meat before consuming a dairy product (and, after consuming a dairy product before eating meat). Packaged kosher food bears a label indicating which rabbinical organization has certified it. Unless the hospital has a kosher oven, packaged kosher food should be left in its original wrapping, wrapped again, then heated. It is best to unwrap it in front of the patient. All of this is of great importance to observant patients; but, a Reform rabbi stresses,

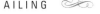

remember that many Jews are not observant. "I know of only two families in our congregation who keep kosher."

Muslims usually prefer *halal* meals, food meeting the requirements of Islamic law; many will insist on this. One Muslim Clinical Pastoral Education student was called upon to teach about this to the food service staff at the hospital in which he was training: "I had to explain what *halal* means, how similar and different it is from kosher, what they'd need to do." Islamic law prohibits all pork products and alcohol (and for some Muslims, shellfish). For some Muslims, it is enough simply to avoid pork. The more observant will want all meat products to be *zabihah,* which means it comes from animals that have been slaughtered in the manner specified by Islamic law. When *halal* food is not available, many Muslims—but certainly not all—find kosher food acceptable, since the standards are similar. In fact, the Islamic Medical Association of North America (IMANA) teaches that this is an option. And, while Islamic law forbids the consumption of blood, blood transfusions are permissible—as IMANA points out.

As with other religious traditions, dietary considerations extend to the content of medications for Muslims. Those which contain alcohol should be avoided unless they are "lifesaving" and no substitute is available. Most Muslims are likely to feel the same about medications containing anything derived from a pig, although one school of legal interpretation asserts that since manufacturing the product causes it to undergo chemical change, this removes it from the category of *haram,* the forbidden. Muslims who are ill are excused from the Ramadan fast. IMANA says that taking medication via a patch or an inhaler does not break the fast, nor does taking a blood test or monitoring one's glucose level (although diabetics would be exempt from fasting anyway).

Sikh law prohibits eating meat from animals killed ritually—which means that observant Sikhs will not eat kosher and *halal* meat and poultry. Beyond that, diet is according to personal preference. Some Sikhs are vegetarians; many are not.

Members of the Bahá'í Faith have no dietary restrictions, and they are excused from the annual Nineteen Day Fast (dawn to sunset from March 2 through 20) if they are ill, pregnant, or traveling. In fact, Bahá'í scriptures emphasize the role of nutrition in maintaining and restoring good health.

Beyond food rules, we have the reality that each culture has its own definition of comfort food. Some hospitals now provide (or allow the patient's family to bring in) these favorites.

Caring for one's hair
Chaplaincy guidebooks often mention Zoroastrian discomfort with having hair brushings or fingernail clippings and such in the room—"any hair, any part of the body that has departed from the body," one doctor explains. A very conservative patient might insist on this, he says. "Nowadays, most people don't care, but in my day, we were very strict!"

Observant Orthodox Jewish women (if married) may wish to keep their hair covered by a wig or scarf. Similarly, many observant Muslim women will want to keep their hair covered with a scarf at all times. "Observant Sikh men (and some Sikh women) want their head never to be uncovered," an educator points out. "They would want to have their head covered at all times, even when sleeping." Even if they remove their more elaborate outer turban, they will still have their hair covered by an "under-turban." Some hospitals have developed a policy of providing sterile, disposable hair coverings for patients who want them. Even a surgical cap might suffice if a scarf is not acceptable to the hospital staff. If a hospitalized Sikh must remove his turban, it should be stored in a respectful way.

Because unshorn hair is an article of faith for Sikhs, questions sometimes arise concerning medical procedures that call for shaving a part of the body. "It varies so much," says one educator. "The very, very strict and orthodox feel very strongly that you should never shave, even at surgery time. In our community, some have brought this up with their surgeons, and I think shaving has been avoided. Surgeons are not generally happy about it, but some have been able to work around it. Other Sikhs are more liberal about it. They think it is not a violation of the cutting of the hair, because it is being done for medical reasons. I've seen it both ways. It has come up more than once."

"I actually was surprised at my own husband," she offers. "My husband is very modern. He's *kesadhari* (that is, he keeps his hair), but he's not *amritdhari* (that is, he is not an initiated Sikh)—and he's a physician! But when he had to undergo a minor surgical procedure, he brought up the hair issue. He wouldn't let them shave him, and the surgery wasn't even on his head! It wasn't anything that was visible. Yet he felt really strongly about it. You never know."

In our post-9/11 environment, American Sikhs are striving to be more clear to others about who they are and what they stand for. "I think that was probably part of it," the educator acknowledges. "My husband may have wanted to make it clear in the public setting of a hospital." In any case, keeping the hair clean and neat is part of Sikh spiritual discipline, so being able to wash, dry, and comb hair (and beard) daily will be appreciated.

Who may care for whom
Buddhist monks and nuns and Hindu renunciates may have taken vows not to touch someone of the opposite sex. Some may have decided these restrictions do not apply in the American context. The head of one Theravada monastery reports that some members of his congregation are surprised that he readily and regularly shakes hands with women, but he does it because hand-shaking is considered the courteous thing to do here. Others may not agree, and for a man to be cared for by female medical personnel (or a woman by a male) may be deeply upsetting to the patient (or to the patient's family or colleagues or congregants), thus compounding an already anguishing situation. It is helpful to ask, and to try to accommodate.

For Sikhs, one woman says, this is a cultural matter. "It is not a matter of the Sikh law code at all." However, observant Jews and Muslims may hold that touching members of the opposite sex is restricted by the law code of their religion. Therefore women (or their accompanying relatives) may insist on being treated only by female doctors and nurses; men, by males. In these matters, however, says one Maryland imam, "the health of the individual takes precedence over the religion." Islamic law allows for otherwise forbidden contact if it is the only way the medical needs of the patient can be met, he explains, although "some Muslims do not understand this."

This reluctance to be touched by a nonrelative of the opposite sex comes up in other aspects of caregiving, one Muslim chaplain notes. "When people are grieving, we have a tendency to want to hug them." While the intention of the person doing the hugging is to offer comfort, we might inadvertently aggravate an already upsetting situation, he explains, by crossing a boundary that might be embarrassing to someone. So, he says, "I would suggest that females hug females, and males hug males."

Reminders of our religion
What might an adherent of one of America's many religions want in his or her hospital room as a reminder of the faith? What about special clothing or devotional objects or ceremonial articles?

Muslim patients may bring a Qur'an, and perhaps a booklet of supplications. Some may prefer to have symbols of other religions removed from their room, or at least covered up.

Bahá'ís might bring a card with the Bahá'í Healing Prayer, or a volume of Bahá'í writings. They might bring a card depicting their nine-pointed star or their ring-stone symbol. The ring-stone symbol's three horizontal lines represent God, God's Messengers, and humanity; the vertical line intersecting them represents the message that links them. Two stars represent God's twin messengers: the Báb and Bahá'u'lláh. Or they might bring a photo of 'Abdu'l-Bahá (Bahá'u'lláh's son).

Jains might bring a picture or image of Mahavira. Their bedside shrine may include a *swastika*—a symbol of *samsara* and the four possible destinations of the soul: the earthly, heavenly, and hellish realms, and *moksha*.

A Hindu may bring a devotional picture of his or her *guru*, or an image of the particular deity he or she venerates, or of Ganesha—the elephant-headed "Remover of Obstacles." Hindu patients may want to keep prayer beads nearby, often in a special cloth bag. Some may want to listen to recorded devotional music. Many find the *Bhagavad-Gita* a source of comfort. Some Hindus mark their foreheads with sandalwood paste or a dot of red or black powder; those who do this daily as an act of devotion may wish to continue their practice in the hospital. Some Hindus wear a "sacred thread"—a knotted string worn over one shoulder and across the torso—which they received during their adolescent rite of passage. They may resist removing it. Likewise, some may wear a necklace, bracelet, or ring as an act of devotion or a symbol of marriage.

"Things of the Shinto shrine really make people feel better," the Reverend Koichi Barrish stresses. "To be able to receive items from the shrine is really very helpful." So a friend or a family member would take those devotional objects to the hospital and put them on the patient's bedside table. "Shinto-followers like to have *omamori* with them," he says. *Omamori* are colorful good-luck charms, often made of silk. Many of them are rectangular (about one-by-two inches), with a drawstring handle. "I always carry one," says a musician. A hospital patient might put it under his or her pillow.

Observant Sikhs wear five articles of faith, and most likely will not want to remove them when hospitalized. These are the Five Ks, so called because the Punjabi name for each begins with the letter *K:* unshorn hair, which observant men and some women cover with a turban; a comb, which traditionally is worn in the hair, under one's turban; a dagger called a *kirpan*; undershorts; and a steel bracelet. Even an infant may be wearing some or all of these symbols. Some Sikhs never remove the undershorts completely before beginning to put on a clean pair. Very conservative patients may become quite upset if caregivers interfere with this practice.

Sikhs may want to bring a *gutka*, the Sikh prayer book, to the hospital. The staff may need help in understanding how this book is to be treated. "Sikhs are very particular about treating the *gutka* respectfully," a businesswoman explains, "because everything in our prayer book is from the *Guru Granth Sahib*, our scriptures. A lot of us will have it wrapped in a little cloth or something. We won't put it on the floor; we won't put it by our feet."

Observant Zoroastrians wear a *sudreh* next to the skin, and may insist on wearing this traditional undershirt under a hospital gown. They also wear a *kushti*, a woolen cord that circles the waist three times. Unless there is no other way to proceed, the *sudreh* and *kushti* should not be cut or destroyed. Those who wear them change these items daily, so a family member will want to bring fresh ones from home. Being allowed to continue to wear these articles of faith while in the hospital may actually benefit the healing process, and removing them forcefully will most certainly be upsetting. "I can say, for example," says one young physician, "that when my grandmother was in the hospital, we asked the staff, 'Please keep her *sudreh* on if you can.' Medical needs are understood as taking precedence over wearing it, though. If you're going to have surgery, there's no way you're going to be wearing your *sudreh* in the operating room! Those things are understood."

"If I were hospitalized," one Vodou initiate indicates, "there might be some traditional things that I would want with me. I might want the beads that were given to me when I was initiated as a priest. Maybe I would want my *paket kongo*—the medicinal packets that were given to me when I became a priest—because that is part of their purpose: they are healing packets. However, I know that I personally would not be too worried about those things unless I was in a critical stage, unless death was at hand."

Devotional practices
Closely related to having articles of faith in patients' rooms is the matter of accommodating their devotional practices. Obviously, prayer ranks high, and often involves some accompanying ritual.

"Our prayers help us find strength in ourselves," a young Zoroastrian physician explains. "Elderly Zoroastrian hospital patients will probably be wearing a *sudreh* and *kusthi*, and will be doing their daily ritual prayers." These involve untying and retying the *kusthi* while chanting. "The *kusthi* prayer is an important part of Zoroastrian prayer, but not the only part. It is a small ritual we do to start off our prayers, and then we continue with other prayer. If one is unable to actually physically tie and untie the *kusthi*, there are many other prayers one could do. Often, patients will be reciting those in their heads. When my grandmother was in a vegetative state, we'd recite prayers to her, because we knew how important they were to her. I am sure that on some level she was saying them in her head. I don't know how much you find the next generations doing that. Our parents definitely are interested that we learn how!"

"Some people I know use prayers on tapes or CDs," she notes. "I know people who play these tapes daily, if they are not able to do the prayers themselves, or no one is around to do them for them." As a gift to the community, Dr. Kersey Antia has recorded a CD of all of the *Gathas*. "Anybody is welcome to have it," he says. "I don't want to sell them; I just want people to be able to use them."

The Sikh holy book includes lots of prayers, a Michigan businesswoman notes. "Now there are people who will find prayers for specific things. That has happened to me so many times. Somebody will say, 'Oh, you're going through this difficulty? Read this *shabad,* and it will be all right.' The literal meaning of *shabad* is "word," she explains. "But when we say *shabad,* we generally mean 'a hymn.' Some Sikhs do believe there are *shabads* that can bring luck. If you ever read any of Yogi Bhajan's material, his answer for every difficulty in life is 'Read the *shabads.*' I just attended a camp with a teacher who said that all diseases can be cured through the Name of God, that you can cure any mind or body disease through meditation and prayer. Does every Sikh believe it? Does everybody use it? No. And is this how *Gurbani*—the Word of the Guru—is supposed to be used? I have my misgivings, but the idea of our scripture being used as a way to get past difficulties in life is very common. I have heard many doctors say they always keep God in mind when they are treating a patient," she concludes. "My cousin is a surgeon, and he says a short prayer right before he does every surgery, because he ultimately wants this to be God's patient. I've heard that more than once."

A Bahá'í oncologist in New Jersey prays about his patients, too. The Bahá'í Healing Prayer hangs on the wall of his office. "The importance of prayer would be very, very important to a Bahá'í," says a Detroit businesswoman. The Bahá'í Faith requires daily ritual prayer, "but there are special prayers that are said about healing—physical, mental, spiritual healing. That would be an important consideration that a Bahá'í would want people in a hospital setting to know—the importance of prayer." On the whole, members of the Bahá'í Faith are quite comfortable with visits from chaplains of any faith, and appreciate readings from scriptures other than their own. However, says one New Yorker, it would have been nice if the Christian doctors and nurses caring for her terminally ill husband had understood that Bahá'ís have prayers, too. "Very often during the day, the chaplain or the nuns would come by and want to pray with him. And so my husband began to talk about the Bahá'í Faith. He said they could pray together, but they just left! That was kind of sad, because the Bahá'í prayers are simply communion with God. I wish that they had stayed and prayed with him."

When their condition allows it, observant Muslim patients will want to get out of bed to make *salat,* the ritual prayer that is to be performed five times a day. Some hospitals arrange for *jum'ah* (communal prayers) to be held in the facility each Friday afternoon. "It's traumatic for Muslims not to be able to make their prayers on time, especially when they are sick," Imam Yusuf Hasan stresses. "It's difficult when you can't wash yourself properly before prayer. Our prayers involve physical movement. When people are ravaged with cancer, they can't do the bowing and the sitting and the standing like they usually do, and that's traumatic for them. But in the Qur'an it says that you can pray lying or sitting or standing. They don't have to make the physical movement. They can even lie in their bed." Do patients sometimes need to be reminded of this? "Definitely," he says.

"I try to teach the medical staff to be sensitive to these issues when they face Muslims," Imam Hasan continues. "I try to let the staff know that at a certain time of day, Muslim patients might be praying. So at those times, it is important to be aware, and not just barge in on patients. Wait until they acknowledge that you are trying to come in and speak with them. If they're not responding, they might be praying! You see? That's one way of trying to be sensitive to an Islamic person who is hospitalized and wants to practice their religion."

"And of course," says a Philadelphia chaplain, "one thing it is sometimes difficult for hospital patients to figure out is, Where is the *qiblah*? In what direction should I make my *salat*? So," she recommends, "if you are likely to take care of Muslim patients in a hospital, carry a compass!"

"Another thing," notes a Michigan graduate student: "a patient's Muslim visitors might still be at the hospital when prayer time comes around. So it is good that many hospitals now have reflection rooms where Muslims can make *salat.* The hospitals around Detroit have copies of the Qur'an in their reflection rooms. People can go there and pray, and read Qur'an for a while, then come back upstairs. That has been a great accommodation."

"I do a class for hospital caregivers," says one imam, "to give them tips on how to interact if they have Muslim patients. For example, Muslims cannot pray through an intermediary to God. There are Christians who have to pray 'in the name of Jesus.' So when they go to pray at the side of the Muslim, they should first ask, 'May I pray with you?' Some might say yes; some might say no, because they believe that only one of their *shaykhs* or someone like that can pray with them. Just recognize that, and respect that, and go on. If they do say yes, then just pray to God, and that's it. To say 'in the name of Jesus Christ' would be offensive to a Muslim, because we don't pray 'through' Jesus. It would be offensive to a Muslim to pray 'in the name of Muhammad.' We pray directly to God."

"There is a prayer that's said for sick people three times a week," an Orthodox rabbi points out, "but if somebody wanted, they would say it more often. It's called the *Mi Sheberach:* 'May God, who blessed our ancestors Abraham, Isaac, and Jacob, bless this person, and heal him or her in body and spirit.'" Traditionally, a hospital chaplain explains, "it is said in the synagogue while the Torah is being read, and is meant to be a communal prayer only. But the *Mi Sheberach* has been 'democratized' in a way. There are some people who still will only say it in synagogue with the religious community in place, but there are a lot of people who know that prayer from synagogue and want to say it at the bedside."

"Singing the *Mi Sheberach* is one thing I like to do when I make hospital visits," says a Reform cantor. "There was also a man in our congregation who was receiving hospice care in his own home. Near the end of his life, he asked me to come and sing to him every day. So I came and sang different settings of psalms for him. That was a powerful experience for me, because he told me exactly what I could do for him. It was a favor this dying man did for me."

Jews should visit the sick just as God visited Abraham during his recovery from circumcision. "We Jews have a long tradition of *bikur cholim*," a chaplain explains. "That is, we are commanded to visit the sick. There is an understanding that when we visit the sick, we take away one-sixtieth of the suffering. So our visiting makes a physical difference to the sick person. There's a recognition that God cares very much about our physical circumstances, and that we have to care about one another's physical circumstances. And the connection of the community through *bikur cholim* has a radical impact on health."

"There are laws about when to visit and when not to visit," she continues. "Not too early in the day, not too late—these are times when there are a lot of gross things going on internally. You are to respect the privacy of the individual, so that he or she would not seem disgusting in his or her own eyes."

"The kind of care *bikur cholim* groups provide really is about the whole life of the individual," the chaplain notes. "This is very different from professional chaplaincy. There is a tradition of physically helping someone who is suffering—even sweeping the floor. There are some pretty remarkable *bikur cholim* groups who will do everything you need. Say there's a child in the hospital. The *bikur cholim* group will provide respite care so the parents can spend a night at home. They'll provide transportation for the kids to and from school if their parents are at the hospital, or they'll provide bus service to various hospitals or doctor visits. Or they'll provide food. Some *bikur cholim* groups even drop off homemade chicken soup! When I was about to give birth, the *bikur cholim* provided a kosher refrigerator so that when I was admitted there would be kosher food right there. One *bikur cholim* group, Chai Lifeline, started Camp Simcha for terminally ill children."

Along with providing for a kosher diet, "the biggest issue in terms of helping Jews feel welcome in a hospital is taking

Shabbat observance into account," a Jewish chaplain explains. "My first daughter was born in a hospital that was very sensitive to Jewish needs. When I said to the nurse, 'I can't leave on Saturday; do you mind if I stay until Saturday night, when *Shabbat* is over?' she said, 'No problem.' That's a welcoming environment. I didn't have to justify, I didn't have to pay extra, I wasn't an alien creature. She knew what *Shabbat* was. That's the whole issue: translating the culture and the laws, and making accommodations."

Since use of electricity is prohibited on the *Shabbat,* observant Jews are not likely to turn their room lights on or off, but most appreciate the nursing staff offering to do that for them. Such a patient might refrain from using the call button during this twenty-five-hour period. Since they are to refrain from writing on the *Shabbat,* they will not want to fill out menu requests or any other forms during that time. Some hospital patients appreciate being provided somehow with a *Shabbat* service. One Conservative rabbi videotaped the service in his Midwestern hospital chapel every Friday for well over a decade. "People could come to chapel to watch the video, or they could watch it in their rooms."

And also, some Jewish patients do the daily prayers, and having the staff know about that practice and at what times those patients might be praying is very helpful. "I worked in a Jewish hospital, and it had a prayer service every day, three times a day," a Conservative rabbi recalls. "Patients could come and participate if they were able, and many doctors participated. This is quite nice. But it was Orthodox, so as a woman, I wasn't able to be in the room, which was hard. It's not easy to accommodate all Jewish needs. Probably people need to know that! If you're accommodating *some* Jewish needs, it doesn't mean you're accommodating *all* Jewish needs."

For example, an observant Jew who wishes to say daily prayers using a *tallit* and *tefillin* (the traditional prayer shawl and *phylacteries*) may appreciate not being disturbed while doing so. On the other hand, others are disturbed if they are *expected* to do so. A Reform rabbi recalls a boy from her suburban congregation who was a patient in a hospital that happened to have a Jewish chaplain. "This rabbi visited the child and gave him some sort of blessing—and then he had him wrap *tefillin*. What was fascinating to me is that this wasn't offered; it was imposed! This child was not happy with the experience. I think it had a lot to do with his concept of who he was—that, as a Reform Jew, he should be making choices."

Some Buddhists speak of praying, but are more likely to practice meditation. "In Buddhism we talk about 'no self' and letting go of your ego, and non-attachment, realizing the interconnection of all things—which is all great," says the Reverend David Zuniga. "But then there is always the question: How do we do that? How do we let go? For me, as a Zen monk, the skillful practice is meditation. I actually do a lot of meditation with terminally ill patients and their families." "A Buddhist patient might welcome a quiet room for meditation or quiet chanting," a Michigan Zen leader adds. "Today most hospitals have a chapel that a person can use."

Actually, one young leukemia patient did a great deal of meditation right in her hospital bed, her father reports. Her chaplain or family would guide her. "When I say that we meditated, I don't mean that we sat silently for hours on end. Usually it involved chanting a mantra. Often we used the Loving-kindness Meditation. Our daughter really enjoyed that."

"When Buddhists are in the hospital, sometimes they are very happy if monks visit them, to bless them," says a Theravada monk. The community knows this. They inform us monks when a person is sick." As a native of Sri Lanka, he also pays pastoral visits to any Sri Lankan Americans who are admitted to the local hospital, regardless of their religion. "If I come to know about them, I go to visit them. That is for friendship."

Like Buddhists, many Jains like a private time for meditation when they are hospitalized, an internist explains. If they are approaching death, she suggests, "they may like someone to come by their bedside and say some prayers for them. In this country, we don't have our Jain monks and nuns, but there are laypeople who can come. Many times it would be a family member or a friend. In my hospital we are very open to this."

"You should let the body help you," a biochemist suggests, "but don't feel you must entertain the senses. You don't need to use your eyes to see beautiful things. Instead, close your eyes and meditate on the *atman,* the soul inside. You need to be in a quiet place so that a sense organ can take you inside instead of outside." In a hospital situation, getting the staff to let the patient have quiet would be an important thing. "Yes," she concurs. "If they hear anything, they should hear only the Jain chants." Jains might therefore prefer hospice for a terminally ill person, she notes, because it allows more control over such things.

"The main Jain prayer is the *Navkar Maha Mantra,*" a Chicago physician reminds us. "The meaning of it is also very powerful. It is something we chant and try to feel through every cell of our body. It can help with the healing. Whatever the outcome, it is more about the healing of the being." The body might die, but the being would still be healed. "That's the main focus," she says. "We also have other prayers that enhance and abate all suffering and illness. We don't pray *to* the *tirthankaras* in terms of asking them for things. We pray so that we can imbibe their qualities and are able to liberate ourselves from the material world."

America's First Peoples, for a host of reasons, are often quite uncomfortable with non-Native approaches to medical care, as we've heard. Things go more smoothly when their healthcare professionals accommodate their traditional practices. "When I had to have surgery," a Keetoowah author explains, "I found a doctor who was used to working with all kinds of people. So I said, 'Can I have a ceremony in the pre-op room?' She said, 'Whatever you want, we'll do it.' So that's what I did. I went to the hospital with my three best friends, a medicine-woman who is also a really good friend, and a medicine-man. The staff realized we'd need a bigger cubicle, so they gave us a private area that could accommodate all of us. My doctor told me that to this day the hospital staff keeps saying that it was the only time that their department felt totally peaceful and calm! When they wheeled me to the operating room, they let the whole group walk me down the hall. While I was in surgery, my friends went up on the roof and had a pipe ceremony, which of course resulted in smoke. Someone called the fire department. The firemen came and said, 'You can't do that up here,' and my friends said, 'Well, we're done,' and that was the end of it.

Someone stayed with me the whole time, because in our culture, we don't leave people alone. No one should go to the hospital alone."

Spiritual Caregiving

Many American hospitals employ official spiritual caregivers in the form of board-certified chaplains, many of whom are ordained, though not all. These chaplains are specially trained to help people negotiate the spiritual chaos of illness and are expected to work ecumenically and interreligiously. The vast majority of these are Christians, though a growing number are Jews. In recent years, a handful of adherents of other religions have earned certification as chaplains. Most credentialed chaplains are certified by the Association of Professional Chaplains (which is multifaith), but there are Catholic and Jewish boards as well.

Imam Yusuf Hasan, the first Muslim affiliate of the Healthcare Chaplaincy and the first Muslim certified by the Association of Professional Chaplains, wishes more Muslims would sign up for Clinical Pastoral Education (CPE). He wants the Islamic community to understand that chaplaincy has a clinical component, which CPE teaches through actual hands-on experience with the medical staff. "You can always go in and read the Qur'an to your patients; you can always go and pray with them; you can lead the *jum'ah* prayer with them. But can you meet them in their hurt? Can you say it's okay to be angry and upset? Those kinds of feelings CPE teaches us to deal with."

Abdullah Antepli, associate director of Hartford Seminary's Islamic Chaplaincy Program, recalls, "Not only was I the only Muslim in my CPE group, I was the only Muslim in the whole Pastoral Care Department of a twelve-hundred-bed trauma center and general hospital! I was very well received by the professional people. At the same time, it was quite challenging because I ended up being the spokesperson for all Islamic and

Muslim issues. I just wanted to be a regular CPE student and do my own work, but I was expected to answer questions from staff and patients about why there's so much violence in the Middle East, and what's going on in Palestine and Israel, and what's happening to Afghani women, and the literacy rate in Indonesia, and Islam's dietary rules. As time went on, I got better at not being defensive. I got better at reminding people that I was there to deliver pastoral care."

Chaplain Antepli cared for Muslims, of course, but his patients also included Jews, Hindus, Buddhists, and "all sorts of streams of Christians." While there was an occasional painful exception, most of them were happy to have his visits. "They had never thought there *were* any non-Christian chaplains. People's perceptions of hospital chaplains are really interesting. The majority think they are just priests sitting in the chapel, waiting for a customer. Most don't realize they are on the floor all the time, providing pastoral care and support."

The role of a hospital chaplain is indeed a little different from that of a congregational rabbi, a Conservative Jewish educator explains. "When I am on a hospital staff as a chaplain, I am there to help you navigate whatever spiritual chaos you may be experiencing, and give you access to religious resources that you may not be able to access for yourself. One of my cherished stories of my time as a chaplain concerns an elderly patient who was a Hassidic rabbi and a Holocaust survivor. He was having trouble putting on his *tefillin* for praying. I made a contract with him that I would come and help him on the days when he didn't have his grandson available to help him. Being a Conservative woman rabbi, sitting with this man, helping him put his *tefillin* on and off, was a concrete task but it was also a way of saying to him that what was sacred to him was sacred to me. It was a way of saying that his frailty would not stop him from accessing God in the way in which he was accustomed, and that I would go out of my way to help him be whole in his spiritual life."

"I'll never forget the day before his last day," she says. "I asked him if he wanted me to come and help him. He said, 'Well, my grandson will be coming.' So I said, 'Then I should say goodbye, because I won't be coming tomorrow.' But he said,

'Well...you *could* come tomorrow.' So I came, and as I was there, I realized that he wanted to introduce me to his grandson, that it was very important to him for his grandson to see who had been helping him with his *tefillin*. It was a way of bringing the Jewish world closer together, and that was part of his spiritual life as well. Jews can be so fragmented. One of the things that can happen in the hospital is that people can become known in ways that don't happen in their regular lives. This rabbi and I could talk to one another in ways that helped him tell his story. He didn't really need to tell his family in the same way, because they had known him for so long. But having a new audience was different! It had a healing power to it."

Across the spectrum of America's religions, we also find congregational leaders and laypersons who are not board-certified chaplains, but who take responsibility for providing spiritual care when a member of their religion-community is ill. "To my knowledge, there are no Buddhist chaplains in our area," says a Michigan Zen practitioner. "I am involved with a program that provides visits for Buddhists who are hospital-bound or in nursing homes or retirement homes."

Helping a family who seeks prayers as they deal with illness is a regular part of the life of a Zoroastrian priest in America, Dr. Kersey Antia stresses. "We do it all the time. Sometimes American Zoroastrians don't know the prayers. So I tell them what to pray. If they don't have the prayers, I copy them and mail them." The Chicago community has a *darbe mehr* (a community prayer hall). "Every Sunday, about noon for a couple of hours, we have a priest available there for any prayers," he explains. "If somebody is sick, someone will ask the priest to pray for the sick person." However, it is not the Zoroastrian practice to summon a priest to the hospital to pray *with* someone, he says. "A hospital is not a ritually pure place, and we are so over-conscious of purity that if a priest goes to a hospital, he has to take a bath afterward."

When they are ill, people may come to the Shinto shrine near Seattle to ask for a prayer or ceremony, says the Reverend Koichi Barrish, the head priest. Someone might also come to ask for a healing prayer or ceremony on behalf of someone else. "That happens all the time as well," he notes. "A large part of our work is doing such things. We have many ceremonies for recovery of health. It's a standard case to pray for someone, whether they are here or not. There are a couple of different forms and many variations for such prayers."

"There's a special Shinto prayer called the *Byoki-heyu,* which means healing of sickness," a young New York priest explains. "A special *Norito* prayer exists for sickness, but each priest has to be creative. Priests have to add their own words. They can fit the prayer for the occasion. This *Norito* prayer was for a baby who was one year old," she explains, holding up a beautiful folded paper with Japanese characters on it. "She was sick. I created this part," she explains, pointing to a section in the middle of the text. "I prayed that she would be healed, that the medicine would help, that the doctor would help. In offering this prayer, I chant in the ancient Yamato language, not common modern Japanese." To whom is the prayer addressed? "To the *kami* who is in residence in the shrine here," she replies. "And of course it reaches the baby's ancestors, too."

This priest says she has never been asked to visit a patient in a hospital in order to say prayers. "People normally come to the shrine here in my apartment. For the Shinto priest, it is better to do prayers where the *kami* is. If someone needs help, if someone needs prayers, I can pray *here* for someone in the hospital." On the other hand, Reverend Barrish does do hospital visitations. He might recite the same recovery-of-health prayers he would offer at the shrine. However, because there are very few Shinto priests in America, he receives hundreds of requests by letter and e-mail to perform ceremonies by proxy—which he does at the shrine. "It's really very helpful. People like to know, even if they are far away, that a ceremony has been done on their behalf—that the *kami* of the divine world have been informed of the situation in a very formal way."

"Jews will want to take advantage of the best available agreed-upon medicine," Rabbi Blanchard asserts, "but they are going to see it as part of a larger process." Jews who are affiliated with a synagogue will be added to that community's prayer list, and will be remembered in daily prayer. In some cases, he says, "the community might even hold a special meeting, and invite everybody to come and say prayers for their recovery." While

Judaism certainly makes room for spontaneous supplications, he explains that "when we get a group together, we're going to go with a set prayer. Traditionally, *tehillim*, psalms, are at the center of our healing ritual. There is still a tradition that, if a person is sick, the community will divide up the psalms, and you commit yourself to reciting a psalm (or more than one psalm) on behalf of the sick person."

Christians who are hospitalized during their holiday seasons can expect to find festive decorations and perhaps a visit from a troupe of carolers to help them through, but patients from other religion-communities have more of a challenge when it is a special time of year for them. During Passover, Jewish patients might appreciate a *seder*. If the hospital permits, their rabbi and family can help with this. Similarly, if hospitalization overlaps one of the Hindu festival periods, friends and family may want to bring the patient sweets or fruit that has been blessed during temple rituals. It would be likewise for Sikhs or Buddhists or anyone else who takes his or her religion seriously. "I have a Christian friend who is a hospital chaplain in Chicago," a Hindu professor says. "She'll take me out to lunch and ask me about different Hindu rituals and festivals. Then, when there is a Hindu patient in her hospital, she'll go and celebrate with them—whatever they want. For instance, she'll try to put up *Diwali* decorations when it is *Diwali* season." Having such reminders of where we are in our religion's annual cycle of celebrations can be healing, and the growing availability of multi-faith calendars makes it easier for caregivers of other religions to help make this possible.

Questions that make a difference

"Maybe it's all right for these manuals to err on the side of conservativeness," says a Sikh educator, "but sometimes it leads to backlash. It's great to make people sensitive to diversity, but you don't want to make them sick of it." A Sikh nurse adds, "Our hospital guidebook on patient preferences stresses a very important point. Even though we have been given a general guideline, each person, each family member still has to be asked, 'Is there anything we can do at this time? What would you like us to do?'"

"Many medical schools, including the one where I teach, are trying to educate our future physicians about appreciating diversity and understanding different cultures," stresses Dr. Humayun Chaudhry, of the New York College of Osteopathic Medicine, where symposia about various religions are part of the required curriculum. "We try to give the students a flavor for what is out there when we actually go into practice. We want more future physicians from our medical school to be cognizant of the different ways in which people express their spirituality. The message I try to get across to our students is to make sure, as they are dealing with an illness, that they make an effort to understand the patient's spirituality, and how patients perceive their illness. Something that is terminal may not necessarily be a negative thing—depending on the person's faith. We always make a point that you should never stereotype. Whether people labels themselves Jewish, Hindu, Christian, Muslim, Buddhist is useful information, but each person reacts to that label differently, and interprets that label differently. We try to educate our future physicians to be aware, and to ask questions."

Asking a simple question can make all the difference, a Buddhist chaplain agrees. "Recognizing the extraordinary variety within religions is so important. I think we can get ourselves into trouble by presuming a lot about people based on a very simple label like 'Buddhist' or 'Muslim' or even 'Protestant'! I think the single most important thing when dealing with any patient, no matter what their religion, is just to ask: 'What gives you meaning? What helps you cultivate equanimity or joy amidst all this difficulty that you're dealing with?'"

"One of the things about being a chaplain is that you're not a doctor, you're not a nurse," he reminds us. "A lot of times there is not something 'practical' that you can do; you can't cure their illness. On the other hand, there are things you can do that are in some ways the *most* practical things: providing spiritual guidance, sitting with people, helping them find their own answers to suffering."

Because it has a decidedly Christian origin, the term "chaplain" is off-putting to some patients. Spiritual caregivers who take pains to respect and support the religious concerns and traditions of others are frustrated when they are perceived as being present merely to proselytize. Some even wonder if another title could be found for the job they do. Even so, there is an upsurge of interest among followers of religions other than Christianity to become chaplains, along with an eagerness in disaster response organizations and many urban hospitals to have chaplain corps that are truly multireligious. "Much of what chaplains do," one Muslim notes, "is what Sufism has taught me about spiritual friendship." Indeed, when grappling with loss of health, enjoying spiritual friendship can mean a great deal.

"To be able to help people in different religions—it's akin to being multilingual," a Buddhist chaplain says. "Cultures are different, words are different, philosophies are different, texts are different. A lot of chaplains go into this work because they want to win souls for their religion. That's absolutely *not* what being a chaplain is about. It's about being a resource for that person— whether they are Christian, atheist, agnostic, Hindu, Muslim. In Buddhism, we have this idea of stepping out of the limiting 'I' constraint that we impose upon ourselves. I try to step outside of my own beliefs, conceptions, desires; I try to have what Buddhists call 'emptiness'—so that I can be there one hundred percent for another person. And I believe that's spiritually possible."

When we wish to understand how the various religions of our neighbors help them understand health and illness, it is important to talk about experiences of hospitalization and medical treatment with people of deep religious faith, and to hear how they bring what is necessary for their soul into the process of what is necessary for their body. "When we invoke spirituality," says physician Jill Baron, "we have to be careful not to offend patients." There will be a range of opinion about what is necessary. It may be next to impossible to accommodate everyone's desires, and health professionals must also observe the many rules and regulations the American medical system imposes. Yet, she stresses, "we have to be aware of where our patients are coming from. Spirituality is not measurable or tangible; it can't be quantified. We need more research into how to evaluate the intersection of religion and medicine." Decisions about life-extending measures often sharpen our focus on this intersection. We turn now to some of these.

CHAPTER THREE

Postponing Death, Extending Life

"DEALING WITH IMMINENT DEATH heightens and magnifies all of the issues people already have," says a chaplain at a Houston cancer center. "Around this one patient, a hurricane of family stuff was going on, but he was an amazingly calm eye of the storm. On what turned out to be his last night, he and I had a long talk, just one-to-one. He said to me, 'My family is all freaked out about what is going to happen to me, and what they can do to keep me alive and make it better. This one wants one thing done; the other wants something else. As far as I'm concerned, I've had a wonderful life, but now I'm looking at a door, and on the other side of it is an even greater adventure. When I am done here, I just slip through that door and go on to see what's possible next. I am completely at peace with that.'"

Thanks to a host of technological developments in recent decades, "one thing" and "something else" include a range of options: dialysis, respirators, portable oxygen therapy, transplantation of body parts, and so on. Decisions must be made. Does any religion's sacred scripture address these decisions directly? Almost without exception, no. However, every religion does provide its adherents with principles on which to draw in facing them. In this chapter, we'll hear some of this reasoning as we take a look at two complex issues: use of life-extending technology (particularly respirators), and whether to be an organ donor or recipient.

Life-Extending Technology

When it comes to taking advantage of the technology modern medicine makes available, usually it is not so much a matter of whether to use the technologies as it is of to what extent they should be used and when to stop their use. When a religion teaches that life is cyclical and we will have another chance, or that death is something akin to changing one's clothes since the soul simply moves from one body to another, or that a more glorious new stage of existence awaits, then does prolonged use of artificial life-support make sense?

"Ten years ago, I broke my skull," says an Ohioan. "I was unconscious; I had amnesia; I had brain damage. So, why did this happen? As a Hindu, it was easy to explain it to myself as well as to my mom. Notions of rebirth and *karma* put a certain perspective on pain, suffering, and death." In this case, life-sustaining technology was used, and he recovered. His brain now works just fine—but what if he had not responded? "This is just one time around; I'll have another chance, and maybe it will be a better chance. So don't keep me alive. If I'm really in bad shape, let me go. I believe life on this earth will happen again for me anyway."

"We strongly believe that when your time comes, you're going to pass," says a Hindu engineer in Louisiana. "Most of our elders tell us, 'Pull the plug if I have to go through circumstances where I am like a vegetable. Please let me go. I have led a full life.' The *Bhagavad-Gita* says that the soul never dies. The body is not immortal. The body is going to go away. You have to leave the body. In our community, when parents are in that situation, most people decide to let them go."

"When someone decides to use life-support, that's when our whole Jain philosophy should come into play," a family physician cautions. "There are times when these methods are really going to help a patient recover from acute illness. But one cannot depend on machines to prolong life beyond reason. We doctors can help the family realize what the situation may be."

"As I see it," says a Jain pediatrician, "when we are born, we have just so many breaths; just so many heartbeats. This is what we are taught. That is our destiny. Maybe modern science tells you that we can extend life by putting somebody on a machine. But the body may die the very next day anyway; or, without being put on the machine, it may live for six months. We cannot predict. If it is time to go, we are going to go. That's how I feel."

This brings us to one of Jainism's cardinal principles: *aparigraha* (non-attachment). For many Jains, there is little to be gained from being overly attached to life. "When life cannot sustain itself," says a Chicago biochemist, "then it is moving into the process of the next life." From a Jain point of view, it should be allowed to do so. That is where the Jain custom of choosing to let go of life comes into play. "When they are very, very sick," an internist explains, "and they know there is not too much doctors can do, some Jains will decide, 'Okay, now I am going to give up eating.'" The practice is known as *santhara*. One makes a vow of total abstinence from food, then fasts unto death, prayerfully and reverently.

"We had a wonderful friend whose ninety-five-year-old grandfather chose *santhara*," another Jain physician recalls. "He said, 'Enough. I am ready to go. I am going to go.' So everybody said goodbye. He said, 'Death is coming, and I am ready for it.' He accepted it, and he died after two or three weeks." Force-feeding or sedating such a patient would be seen as doing violence to the ideal of dying while meditating, concentrating totally on one's spiritual destiny.

Santhara is not a common practice, though, even among Jains in India. Nevertheless, as the biochemist explains, "I have been researching it, and have been preparing my dad and my brother. When I went to India recently, I brought back some information on how it is done. A few months ago, we talked about how you perform this ritual, and that night, my dad went to a low stage of energy. So we all sat around and said prayers. He woke up in the night and saw us all sitting around, saying prayers, and he said, 'Oh, this is good rehearsal!'" This is a custom that requires mental preparation. "The idea is that you let go of your soul," she explains. "Someone who has good ego strength and spiritual strength can do something like this, and not be afraid of death."

"Sikhism says that each person's duty is to do the best we can," an intensive-care nurse observes. "It is a person's individual decision whether to use life-extending technology. There are so many instances when you use technology, and still the life is not extended. It kind of says that if the person has to die, he will die regardless. Many Sikhs really believe that there is nothing wrong with death. Death should be welcomed. It's a chance to meet God! So, my parents have friends who, when they were at that stage, said, 'Well, if I need to be intubated or put on life-support for a small period (a week or two) that's okay, if it's just to get over a little hump. But don't keep me alive like that indefinitely, because I am comfortable with the fact that I have to die.' It is very individual."

"There is no unanimous opinion about use of life-extending technology by Zoroastrians," Dr. Kersey Antia indicates. "I was taught that the dead have no right over the living. That's why, when we die, we have no right to occupy any land, and why no wood should be burned for us. Land belongs to the living. Similarly, with medical decisions, you have to consider the outcome. If, on the whole, there is no chance that the person will recover, wasting things just to sustain life on respirators is not in conformity with Zoroastrian principles. The person's soul will just be confused between the two worlds." God determines the length of our lives, he says. "We should accept that and not rebel against God by prolonging death unproductively, and certainly not at the expense of others. If you want to keep someone alive for a day or two, so that the son or daughter could travel to be there at the end, I guess that could be worthwhile. We can use or abuse modern methods of surviving."

Some Buddhists make it clear that they do not want any artificial life-support used on them. It might interfere with their *karma*, they argue. "I don't want to prolong my life with those machines for an unnecessary period of time," says a Theravada monk. "If you can reasonably see that it is not going to work, what is the point of keeping the person on the machine? People who are living are suffering because of you. I don't want that to happen. Some of the people in my community may be sharing the same thoughts."

"The Buddhist attitude is not to cling to anything," a Zen teacher points out. "This doesn't mean that you don't have close relationships with people who are important to you. But there is a difference between grabbing onto them and just being with them. Buddha taught us that one of the reasons we experience self-induced suffering is that we cling to things. We cling to what we like, and push away what we don't like. Clinging is one of the reasons that we suffer. In fact, clinging to life is something a Buddhist attempts to avoid. Dying is the normal cycle of the process, so when it's time to go, it's time to go."

But as one Buddhist medical ethicist reminds us, classical Buddhist teachings make a distinction between accepting the inevitability of death when further treatment (or nourishment) clearly would be pointless, and rejection of medical care with the intention of ending one's life. Life need not be preserved at all costs, but neither may one "make death one's aim"—for that would violate Buddhism's First Precept: Do not kill. This is why any number of Buddhists have campaigned against legalization of euthanasia, and instead have been enthusiastic supporters of hospice care for the terminally ill.

A *person* is that which occupies a body between conception and death, he asserts, and, according to classic Buddhist texts, when the body no longer has vitality, heat, and self-awareness, death has occurred. The body of someone in a persistent vegetative state still has two of these three indicators, so such a patient remains worthy of compassion and the basic necessities of life. So, in this ethicist's opinion, someone with irreversible brain injury remains a person, just as does a patient with serious injury to some other organ.

"In Buddhism, we say that *samsara* and Nirvana are one," explains a Zen monk in Texas. "Suffering and joy exist together. There is always this dual edge to everything in existence. We can do amazing things medically that we couldn't do even ten years ago. But the shadow side of that is that we sometimes push far too aggressively for care and then we really cause suffering. There are also funding issues around end-of-life care, and the fact that technology helps to isolate us. Sometimes in rural areas, people may not have the medical technology we have in our big cities, but they really care for the terminally ill person in a very fine way."

End-of-life issues present another case of the Jewish attempt to negotiate irresolvable tensions, Rabbi Tzvi Blanchard observes. "In illness there is a tension between the desire for the quick cure and the recognition that the illness is part of a larger process with which you have to come to terms. The dying process is the same way. The key here is in the title of my book: *Embracing Life and Facing Death*," he continues. "When you first start, you know you're ill. Because you're life-oriented, you put everything you can into embracing life. And all the metaphors work that way: 'We're going to fight this thing; we're going to beat this thing.' But you know that if it doesn't work, at some point you will actually have to change your attitude. You realize: It's not going to work; I'm not going to live. Once that reality is owned, then the debate starts."

In Judaism we find the notion of *pikuach nefesh*—preservation of life. "Life itself is seen as valuable," Rabbi Blanchard explains. "That doesn't mean that you preserve it at all costs. That's a different story. But you don't have to prove that life is worthy of value from the viewpoint of classical Jewish bioethics, and for most contemporary Jewish bioethics as well. So the question is, What to do? That depends on the circumstance."

"Chaplains facilitate decisions," says a Conservative rabbi. "Jews will often refer to authoritative rulings from within their own community. The Orthodox world, the Reform world, the Conservative world all post teachings about whether someone should disconnect from life-extending equipment, and how. The role of the chaplain is to help the patient be knowledgeable and make good decisions, but if he or she is active in a congregation, the home rabbi would convey the authoritative teaching of that movement. Many Jews are unaffiliated, yet still want to do something in the Jewish tradition."

Some Jewish ethicists see in the Talmud a notion that, just as one should not hasten death, neither should one postpone it artificially with feeding tubes, respirators, and other heroic measures. Others might see feeding and hydration of the terminally ill as justifiable, but not the use of a respirator. "Let's put it this way," says a Modern Orthodox educator. "There's a difference between not putting someone on a respirator in the first place and taking someone off. And there is a difference between not putting someone on a respirator and not feeding them. So, a 'Do Not Resuscitate' order would be far more acceptable than unhooking life-support." Human beings obviously need food to survive, but one Conservative Jewish ethicist argues that nutrition given via a tube is "medicine" rather than food. Like any medicine, it makes sense to give it to the patient as long as there remains reasonable expectation of recovery. If recovery cannot be expected, then the dying process should not be prolonged. Other rabbis counter that food is food—no matter how it is delivered.

"When the Terry Schiavo case was in the headlines," Rabbi Blanchard notes, "a major Jewish research center said that there are three conditions under which a person does not have to take medical treatment—which also means you can remove medical treatment for somebody who is unconscious. The first is that this person wouldn't want to be in pain. The second is that this person *is* in pain. The third is that this person's prognosis is only a few months—three to six months, which means that the person is really dying. At that point you don't have to be kept alive in order to suffer pain."

"Again, Jews will always have disputes about this," he admits. "Some people will say, 'Continue all measures unless you're imminently dying.' Some people will insist on resuscitating you even if you're imminently dying. Some would resuscitate if the patient had only three seconds more to live. Then there are groups where they would say, 'You know what? This is futile. Let's see if we can do this without pain,' especially if the person is unconscious. The bulk of opinion will settle in around, 'If I've had a heart attack, let me go. If I'm unconscious, don't give me antibiotics. If I'm in pain, just let this be over. If I'm not in pain, let it go on.' It's not about what your life is worth. It's about why you should have to suffer this pain."

Rabbi Blanchard recounts a classical Jewish story that illustrates this. "Rabbi Judah the Prince is dying. His students are praying desperately for him to live and as a result, God is granting him more life. But his maid knows how much pain the rabbi is in and that he can't get out of bed to do his ritual activities. So she stops praying for him. She goes to the roof, takes a pot, and knocks the pot off the roof. When it breaks, all the students down below are startled. Therefore, they stop praying for a moment; and in that moment, Rabbi Judah the Prince dies! The point of the story, of course, is: Why should he have to suffer that pain?"

The Qur'an makes the inevitability of death quite clear to Muslims, stresses medical ethicist Faroque Khan. However, he notes, "the exact definition of death remains vague. In the Qur'an, God states that he takes away the soul upon the death of the person. Where does the soul reside, and how do we—as health providers and lawyers—determine that at the bedside? In the less technologically advanced countries, this dilemma does not exist since most deaths occur in homes where, in the absence of artificial devices, nature takes its course and death is relatively easy to recognize."

"In 1963 in my home in Kashmir," Dr. Khan recalls, "as a medical student I was asked to evaluate 'Grandma, who didn't look good.' With my rudimentary clinical skills, I listened for the heartbeat. Hearing none, I put a strip of cotton under Grandma's nostril and, seeing no movement, declared her dead in the absence of heart sounds and breathing. Grandma was laid to rest. Fast forward to the year 1999. As chief of medicine in a busy hospital in New York, I would have a much harder time declaring someone dead who is being ventilated on a machine and shows some traces of heartbeat on the attached cardiac monitor, but is unresponsive. In a Kashmiri home, it was relatively easy for me to declare that the Creator had separated Grandma's body from her soul; it not so easy today in the hospital settings in the USA."

"As a physician caring for critically ill patients in New York," he continues, "I reviewed the various Islamic definitions of death and concluded that using cortical and brain stem death as criteria of death is quite acceptable in Islam. In approaching potentially controversial issues such as end-of-life care, as a Muslim I take into account what is the most appropriate action under the circumstances. While *Shari'ah* protects each individual's life, religion, mind, property and family, it does in difficult cases provide the option of choosing the lesser of the two evils; and a cardinal principle is that necessity overrides the prevailing rules."

When it comes to end-of-life issues, a Muslim should keep four principles in mind, Dr. Khan suggests: First, do one's best to maintain life. Second, in combating an illness, do not introduce unbearable pain or suffering. Third, look upon hardships as tests from God, remembering that God rewards patience, persistence, and hope in divine mercy. And fourth, remember that treatment ceases to be mandatory when scientific evaluation indicates that it is obviously futile. The patient is still entitled to nutrition, hydration, nursing, and relief of pain, but need not be subjected to extraordinary medical interventions. In fact, IMANA (the Islamic Medical Association of North America) discourages prolonged maintenance on artificial life-support.

"I believe it is Islamically acceptable, and often an act of love," Dr. Khan asserts, "to forgo or withdraw technologies and treatments aimed at prolonging life (ventilation, dialysis, nutrition, hydration) when they offer little reasonable benefit or are an unreasonable burden to the patient." In such a case, he explains, "the disease causes the death; and the person chooses life without the burden of disproportionate medical intervention, thereby accepting the inevitability of the dying process and Allah's will." Not surprisingly, Dr. Khan is an advocate of advanced directives. He believes that Islam permits them, and points out that the Prophet Muhammad himself validated the notion. "He told his followers that anyone who knows that a patient does not want medicine must not force it on him or her."

Chaplain Yusuf Hasan wants Muslims to remember, however, that "life-extending technology was created by God. All is created by God Almighty. We can have no knowledge, except what God gives. God wants us to use these things. Technology is a utility. God wants us to have it, and to utilize it for the betterment of human being."

"Longevity has its place in Islam," he continues. "You know, if you've been doing good all these years, you want to continue to do good, to help humanity. So all this knowledge is for a reason, and if we Muslims have to be on life-support for certain situations, we will be on life-support. The Prophet Muhammad says this: 'None of you should wish for death; but if you wish for death, you should pray, *O Allah, give me life if life is better for me, and give me death if death is better for me.*' That goes back to the quality of life: what would our quality of life be? Now, if I have been in an airplane crash or a car crash, life-support will probably be the best thing for me. But if I have internal organs that are broken down—kidneys and livers and hearts—it wouldn't do me any good to be on life-support."

"As the chaplain, I never tell a patient that they should do this or that," Imam Hasan stresses. "I give them what the Qur'an says, and what the Prophet said and did, and let them make their decision. But I would surely be there to say, 'Look: you have the right to make those decisions.' These persons have a right to the technology that's available. It's unfortunate that many Muslims have mixed their culture with our religion. We need to know how to separate religion from culture. That would help people make a better, more astute, clearer decision."

"Most Muslims see quality of life and quantity of life as one and the same," a Shi'ah critical-care nurse insists, "so we have to push for what others call extreme measures, but we don't see them as extreme. The Muslim mind says that, in suffering, the soul is also growing in wisdom and in grace. There is atonement for anyone who suffers. We don't want to interfere in that domain. We want to alleviate pain, but we are not to confuse that with alleviation of suffering. If we did not suffer, we would not grow."

"But let's say the patient is brain-dead," she continues. "The state has said the patient is dead because brain-death is death, and Muslims have to obey the law of the land. I teach the physicians how to say, 'Your loved one has died,' perhaps by saying, 'The soul has departed and gone to God' even though he or she is still on a ventilator, rather than confuse the family by saying, 'The brain has died.' This absolves the family of responsibility for interrupting the soul's work."

"The Muslim has choice," she stresses, as long as we are prepared on the Day of Judgment to explain to God how we decided what we would do. I have to make my choice; my family cannot make it for me. My mom said to me again last week, 'Don't put me on a ventilator, no matter what!' I had to say, 'Mama, unless it is written down, you are putting me in an awkward position with God. If you want that, you need to absolve me. You need to write that down, so it is you who is saying it—not me on behalf of you.' I can deliver the message, but I can't be the voice."

"It's not only just the technology that's important in Bahá'í Faith," says a Michigan businesswoman. "It really is the spirit and the intent and the well-being of those who are around the person as well." Whether and how long to use life-support technology really has a lot to do with how the patient and the family members are able to resolve this. In July 1985, the Universal House of Justice (the Bahá'í Faith's governing body) ruled that the Sacred Text does not seem to speak to the matter of whether to withhold or remove life-support when a patient is terminally ill, and that the question of whether to uphold the provisions of a patient's living will or not is best left to the conscience of the individual.

Knowing this latitude is available can be comforting to Bahá'ís. "My stepmother was on life-support," explains a Bahá'í Midwesterner. "When it became clear that her lungs could not support her without a respirator and that she had suffered severe brain damage, and that all extraordinary options had been tried, and that all the medical personnel recommended removing life-support, the family met and agreed to let nature take its course. We each individually expressed to her soul our explanations, prayers, and goodbyes. We all were with her as the life-support was disconnected. She passed on peacefully twenty minutes later. We shared a profound sense that we were doing the right thing."

"I've been in this position twice," says another Bahá'í, "with my daughter and my father. My strong belief that 'worlds holy and spiritually glorious will be revealed to your eyes,' and the wonderful principles of eternal life as defined by Bahá'u'lláh allowed me to let them go with joy for their journey. Part of me is still attached to these wonderful people, but I've been able to feel and see a little of where they are. The pain I experienced at their passing was that I could not be there with them—yet."

In the Cherokee tradition, a healer says, "we are taught how we are supposed to behave. We take full responsibility for our actions. Each of us makes our own decisions, and we are responsible for those. No one can take that away from us. We have to look at whatever we have created and deal with it. I think that most Cherokee people would not be interested in extraordinary measures to extend their lives. In fact, I think that most of us would rather die at home. We see death as a private experience."

"Life-extending technology is recent," explains a Vodou priest, "so the ethical issues around it are new in the context of a religion that's hundreds and hundreds and hundreds of years old. It is new in a society where people still have mixed feelings about dying in a hospital. It is new in a community that's an immigrant community, and we've only been here in America— the critical mass of us—for two or three generations. For the bulk of us, we are only confronting these issues now, because it is only now that our parents are beginning to pass away. It is new for our community here, because even the biggest hospital in Haiti would probably never have these things, unfortunately. Going back to what I said about a Vodou notion of person-hood—about the *ti-bon-zanj* and the *gwo-bon-zanj*," she continues, "if you are in a vegetative state, one of these has been taken away from you essentially. You've lost one of those things, and you are incomplete. You are no longer human; you are not a person, in that sense. The quality of one's life is an important thing."

Organ Transplantation

Possibilities for organ transplantation have increased markedly in recent years. Religions have the means, either by appealing to tradition or through scholarly interpretation of sacred texts, to encourage or discourage this medical option. But, as one ethicist cautions, "there are Jewish *text* attitudes, and then there are Jewish *people* attitudes. The range is large." He could be speaking for just about any religion-community. Within their texts and traditions, some members find support for their reluctance; others find reason to encourage organ transplantation emphatically. Here are some examples.

Reluctance
"Many Native Americans believe that when we die, we have to have all our parts with us," a Keetoowah leader comments. "Most traditional people don't like organ transplants," concurs a Mohawk chief. "Most of them will prefer just to go ahead and die, because they don't want to steal somebody's spirit, someone else's stuff. They usually believe you're born with your body, and it has to go back in one piece. Even if you have an amputation, they take that to where you're going to get buried, so later on you will join that. So, with diabetes, it they have to take a leg off, they bury it."

According to traditional Cherokee beliefs, a traditional healer explains, "part of your soul lives in your liver. I don't think many Cherokee people are going to donate their liver!" Or receive somebody else's liver? "Well, I can't say that *nobody* would choose to do that," he replies, "but I think there is a certain level of discomfort with that idea. I think most Cherokee people would not donate their organs, because we think you should be buried intact. I think that, while there will certainly be exceptions, most traditional people would avoid any extreme measures to save their life, so they would prefer not to be organ donors or to receive an organ."

In Vodou, we encounter the notion of *ashé*, a Yoruba term that refers to life, or to the things that represent life-force. "For instance," a priest explains, "when we make offerings, when we make sacrifices, we take the *ashé* of something. And the *ashé* is also manifest in very specific things. It's your liver, your spleen, your lungs, your heart: these organs are your *ashé*. You take away any one of these things, and you're in trouble. It doesn't matter whether you are a rooster or a human being, you need that!" Hence reluctance among traditional Vodouisants to participate in organ transplantation.

Some Muslims do not condone organ donation, because they believe the body should be buried intact. "When the subject of organ transplants first came up a few years ago," recalls a Lebanese-American resident of Detroit, "Islamic scholars discouraged Muslims from participating. They said that the body was to be buried in its totality; and that if during the course of one's life, for health reasons, something had to be removed, *that* should be buried. It shouldn't be cast into a garbage can or into an incinerator. It was part of that person."

"You'll find many Muslims who will not want to donate organs to an organ bank," notes an African-American imam in New York. "Especially the poor people of our society and the people of color. They have seen people like them who need these organs being skipped over—perhaps because they lacked the money or the fame or the insurance or whatever it is."

"A lot of American Sikhs are not comfortable with the concept of organ donation, because we come from India," says an intensive-care nurse. "In India, most people think that everything that is in the body should be burned with you." This makes sense when we think about the Sikh attitude toward "keeping hair": we are to keep what God has given us. "Indeed," she agrees. "You don't give it away. Some Sikhs will say, Okay, I'll give my eyes away, but nothing else."

Organ transplantation is a controversial subject among many Zoroastrians, a Chicago priest explains. "Orthodox Zoroastrians think that we should not disturb the body. They also believe that, not only should we not disturb our own body, but also we should not take anything from another dead body. As soon as the body is dead, it becomes impure, and we don't want to carry something impure in our system. On the other hand, one high priest came here for a visit, and somebody asked him this question. He said, 'No; we shouldn't give anything from our body; but if we want to take from somebody to make ourselves live better, then it's okay.' There are all kinds of opinions."

"Generally, Shinto is not in favor of such things," one priest notes. "Basically, at a certain point, the body just wants to return to nature. At a certain point, the body really wants to decompose. The *mitama* really wants to be on its way. So to fight against that natural parting is against the natural process." Also, there is the concept of *itai*: the ongoing relationship between the person who died and the family and friends left behind. Shinto-followers often are concerned the *itai* will be damaged or disrupted by cutting into a corpse for autopsy or organ-harvesting.

Because Shinto is a life-affirming worldview whose main focus is cleanliness and purity, and since terminal illness and death connote impurity and negativity, Shinto-followers may turn to Buddhism for help in dealing with end-of-life issues, notes Marianne Tanabe, a Hawaiian physician who specializes in geriatric medicine. Or, they simply avoid talking about these things openly. Conversations around informed consent procedures, choices in treatment, and advance directives may be difficult at first, Dr. Tanabe says, and this can get in the way of decisions about the use of life-support, making a living will, or discussion of organ transplants (either as a donor or a recipient). On the other hand, she points out, Shinto can help its followers be matter-of-fact and accepting in their approach to terminal illness, facing it with the traditional assertion, *shikata ga nai*. "The meaning of *shikata ga nai* is 'it cannot be helped.' This view takes any blame or feeling of failure off of the person and his or her family. It embodies an almost stoic acceptance of a difficult circumstance."

Similarly, some Chinese-Americans may be Buddhist (or Christian), yet draw upon aspects of Taoism and Confucianism when thinking about organ donation and reception. Keeping one's body intact may be valued highly—either out of respect for nature (a Taoist concern) or respect for one's parents (a Confucian concern that our parents give us our body, and it is most respectful to return it in the condition it was received). This is increasingly difficult to do, due to modern surgical and medical-technological methods.

Among America's Shinto-followers and Japanese-American Buddhists "the concept of organ donation may not be received well," Dr. Tanabe cautions. "Traditionally," she explains, "organ donation is not favored because of the importance of dying intact, and because the concept of brain-death, as opposed to death occurring 'naturally' when the heart ceases to beat, is sometimes difficult to understand." In cases where a rift develops between those relatives of the deceased who favor organ donation and those who resist this notion, "having persons of authority and knowledge available for education and counseling to the extended family may ease, if not totally prevent, the rift."

The discomfort some Buddhists feel with the notion of organ donation seems to stem from Buddhist understandings of the relationship between the "consciousness" and the physical body. According to classical Buddhist teachings, one medical ethicist points out, a body is dead when it lacks vitality, heat, and self-awareness. When it comes to organ donation, the crucial question is whether the modern notion of brain-death correlates to this ancient formula. Some think it does; others think it does not—reminding us that the Buddha himself was pronounced dead because his attendant could discern no signs of life in him, when in fact the Buddha was really in a deep, deep meditative state.

According to one prominent Buddhist view, even though the five senses shut down upon clinical death, our consciousness still needs time to make its way back to "formlessness," and this takes at least three days after we have breathed our last. Even moving the corpse, much less harvesting organs from it, would disturb a natural process that is critical for rebirth. From a Tibetan point of view, a layman explains, if the deceased was a strong Buddhist practitioner, then the spiritual realizations he or she might achieve during these few days following clinical death have the potential to benefit countless beings for all eternity. That would be far more significant than the short-term benefit organ donation would provide to a few individuals.

Acceptance
Some Buddhists offer a compromise. Wait twenty-four hours, they say; this is sufficient. The tissue and bone of the deceased could still do someone else some good. Or, the body could be donated to medical research. Or, one could elect to be a live donor of bone marrow, blood, or even a kidney. And, one Tibetan Buddhist clarifies, "if you know you *don't* have a strong meditational practice, being left undisturbed after clinical death is not important. By consciously donating your organs, or donating your body for research, you will be making merit with your last act of generosity in this lifetime. It is best to leave some directives. My wife has a donor-sticker on her driver's license; I don't. I'm not sure what I want to do yet. I'd like to do it all: be a donor *and* have a strong meditative practice."

But there is another way to look at it, he points out. "Surviving this present rebirth as long as possible might be the best thing we could be doing, because we don't know what realm we might be thrown into next. The longer we can extend the life we are in now, the more we can cultivate virtuous states of mind. We want to be sure we have a good future rebirth in order to benefit others."

"Now donating organs is something that a Buddhist should be very happy to do," a Michigan Zen teacher asserts. "The body is a vessel, and when you're finished with it, it should be treated respectfully, but yet it is a vessel. So, to donate parts of that vessel which may help someone else is something that is encouraged. There was an Indian monk, Shantideva, who said that the enlightened person should be like a corpse lying in the road for the birds and animals to pick at. He meant that you should give yourself up without attachment, without any agenda. Donating organs certainly almost comes literally to that sense."

What else in the Buddhist teaching might help a Buddhist think he or she *should* donate organs? "The Ten Perfections Stories talk about giving, helping other people," a Theravada monk explains. "Blood donation is part of that also. It is influenced by those stories. I have told people I am going to give my whole body." When a woman in his Staten Island congregation died recently, her family donated her eyes, he notes. "If benefit can be gained from a body that is going to be destroyed anyway, let's use it."

The Reverend David Zuniga agrees. "Organ donation can be seen as a very special Buddhist spiritual practice, because we have the idea of 'no-self.' Your body is *not* who you are. Your body is an efficacious thing, but you can't have attachment to things. You can't cling to things, because things are always changing. In a sense, organ donation is the ultimate act of compassion and non-attachment and non-clinging. In fact, whenever I've talked with Buddhists who are at the end of their lives, they have very much wanted to be organ donors." Interestingly, all of the 239 monks and nuns ordained alongside him have signed up to be organ donors.

Ancient Chinese stories contain many references to organ transplants, even across species, a Taoist priest explains. "A Taoist will totally support, and enthusiastically accept, organ transplantation," he declares. Not all American Taoists are Chinese, he reminds us. Chinese or not, one can embrace Taoism's emphasis on "the natural way" and still take advantage of modern scientific advances. "Taoists always were cutting-edge scientists in China," he asserts.

"I personally feel," a Vodou priest indicates, "that, especially in the African-American community, many of us don't get to live because others of us don't donate bone marrow, we don't donate our organs, we don't give our retinas, we don't leave things behind that can save our community. So, on the back of my driver's license, I have indicated that I am an organ donor. Perhaps within the 'orthodoxy' of my Vodou tradition, I'm not supposed to do that; I should keep my *ashé*. But I've decided, 'Okay, maybe I'll give everything away but my heart.' For myself, I reached this kind of compromise. I cannot honestly say how many Vodouisants have actually thought about it within the realm of Vodou practice, though."

"Hinduism neither prohibits nor endorses organ transplantation," says a nephrologist in upstate New York. "I think it is up to the individual. We Hindus believe that when people die, the soul leaves the body, and the body is nothing but *pancha mahabhuta*—the Five Great Elements of air, fire, earth, water, and ether. With cremation, each element merges into whatever it came from. That will be the end of the body, so whatever you do with it is entirely up to you. The body is disposable, ultimately. But actually, Hinduism teaches us to use the body for the benefit of others while we are living."

A member of an *Arya Samaj* congregation in Michigan would agree. "According to our Vedic scriptures, Hinduism's oldest sacred texts, the definition of *dharma* is to do good to others," he explains. "And in our scriptures there is a saying: 'To do good to others is a virtue; and to make others uncomfortable is a sin.' If you can help the person, that would be the best. We can help others by the body, by the wealth, by the knowledge which we have got." In fact, for many Hindus, donation is an important dimension of *yajna,* fire sacrifice. "'Donation' means to give to others the rights to things which you own, but the only 'payment' one can receive for a donation is appreciation. Donation to save the life of others is the best charity we can make. So it is real love for mankind, and it is also self-sacrifice. By this donation, the body of one person can save many persons, because after death he can donate his eyes, he can donate other parts of his body. So that is what we think about the donation of organs. It is good."

The Bahá'í Faith has a legal tradition, and its governance is conducted by consensus. At the international level, this is provided by the Universal House of Justice, which can make judgments on the relationship of Bahá'í teachings to contemporary issues. In 1946, in response to a question about organ transplants, it indicated that nothing in Bahá'í teachings would forbid a member of the faith to donate his or her eyes to another person, or to a hospital—saying, "on the contrary, it seems a noble thing to do." However, in subsequent decades, it has been reluctant to rule on other kinds of transplants.

Foundational to discussions of organ transplantation, a Michigan businesswoman explains, is the fact that "the Bahá'í writings speak of the body as a temple, the place where the spirit once resided. It is to be treated with utmost respect and dignity, even though there may not be a connection between those two any more—the spirit and the physical body." There may come a time, she suggests, when the Universal House of Justice might examine complexities such as how the time of death is determined when there is a desire to harvest organs. "When is a person alive, and when has a person passed to another world? That question has complexities associated with it that have to do with organ harvesting, or live transplant, or people selling organs—a kidney or other body part—in order to survive economically. These are the kinds of things that, in my opinion, will lead us to a great deal of further discussion, and to further understanding about what it means to donate a body part in the context of the Bahá'í Faith."

Because the Bahá'í writings make clear that, until ruled upon by the Universal House of Justice, one is free to make one's own decision as one's conscience directs, "I personally have indicated that, upon my death, certain organs such as eyes, heart, kidneys, and so on, are to be donated to the living," says one Bahá'í professor. "In such cases, once the organs are removed, the remains must be buried—not cremated."

"My CPE colleagues were really surprised at how progressively Islamic theology treats human beings," says a Muslim chaplain in Connecticut. "Organ donation is commonly accepted. A few small pockets of Muslims reject or question it, but the majority of credible institutions and scholars all over the world say it is an act of charity, that it should be encouraged, and that Muslims should be donors. I am, personally, an organ donor; my wife is; my children are." A New York hospital chaplain agrees. "If a Muslim wants to give an organ, it is considered as giving a gift, and Islam teaches us that we'll get a blessing for giving a gift." However, he says, "some Muslims prefer to donate an organ to a person they know. If they know who the recipient will be, most would be more than happy to donate."

This question has arisen in the Detroit Muslim community as well, one businessman says. "Should we donate indiscriminately? God forbid that we should donate part of our body to preserve a life, and that life was preserved to do evil! What would be the implications for us as human beings in the Hereafter and on Judgment Day? Organ donation should be doing good. But we all know that what we intend to be good might have an adverse effect, not only on the recipient of the organ, but on people who came into contact with that recipient. It's a little like playing God. So it hasn't been easy for Islamic scholars to say, 'No problem. Let's do this on a secular basis. You can put your organ in a bank, and somebody else will direct it.'" Lately, he has heard some scholars say that the donor should have some input into where the body part is going; if that's not possible, they have said, it would be better not to donate. "Again, the complexity of what we are doing is not within the realm of our understanding, so we have to be cautious."

"It is a service to humanity if you can improve somebody's health or alleviate their miseries even after you die. I think this is a core Jain principle," says a Long Island surgeon. As it does with other medical matters, Jainism's principle of *ahimsa* plays a major role in thinking about organ transplantation. "In Jainism, we say that the body is just a vehicle for that soul," a pediatrician reminds us. "The soul determines whether the body is alive or dead. The soul never dies; it just departs from the body. So when the soul has departed, there is no life in that body. The body was there before; the body was there afterwards. But the soul has gone. So when you harvest an organ, you are just taking a part of that vehicle for someone else's body. So you are not really killing something. You're not harming anything."

"At the moment we die and the soul departs," says a Jain family physician, "a process begins that slowly, slowly changes the body so that it becomes inert. During that process, there is only a specific time where that organ can be taken for support of the next body. It's a process, but it's not *life*."

"Life is *chetna*—energy," says a Jain internist. "That's what we're talking about. Energy is soul. It cannot be created or destroyed. The supply of blood vessels and all that is making those organs is all that we are sustaining. We can take someone's organs out and give them to somebody else because there is no cellular death at that point. But the soul has already left."

The Jewish comfort level with organ donation has increased as medical procedures have been refined, an Orthodox ethicist observes. "Now physicians can say, 'Listen. We're not just taking your organ; we can pretty much assure you that it will be used to help someone.' Corneas—we don't have to prove that there will be an immediate need for the cornea anymore, because we're so successful at storing and replanting them. Kidneys, livers, hearts, whatever doctors can use—the success rate is so much higher, people are now more likely to think, 'Okay. Save somebody's life.'"

"Everybody affirms certain transplants," a Conservative rabbi agrees, "like corneas or lungs or liver or kidney—because everybody affirms the principle that God wants us to save lives. The heart transplant is very tricky, because the traditional Jewish definition of death is that you are not breathing. If you are breathing, you're alive. So, if somebody is breathing by means of a respirator, there is a dispute about whether brain-death is an actual Jewish death. The concern with a heart transplant is that you would be killing somebody in order to harvest the heart for somebody else; and Jewish tradition would not allow for that."

"From the earliest days that organ donation became a possibility medically," a Jewish hospital chaplain notes, "the Reform and the Conservative Movements said, 'This is a great *mitzvah;* this is life-saving; this can make a difference.' The Orthodox rabbis were more reluctant. But now even Orthodox rabbis I know have allowed organ transplants, because we can identify that we are saving a life. There is no greater religious obligation than that."

Tzvi Blanchard, an Orthodox rabbi, is a member of the Halakhic Organ Donation Society (HOD). *Halakhic* means "in accordance with Jewish law," he reminds us. HOD is a rapidly expanding group of rabbis (including many Orthodox) who assert that organ donation is in accordance with Jewish law. In fact, an Orthodox medical ethicist points out, a number Jewish legal authorities (including the Chief Rabbinate of Israel) have said that when the brain stem ceases to function, this qualifies as "death," and the organs of this patient may be transplanted, even if the use of a ventilator keeps the heart beating.

"We HOD members allow the use of our names and our pictures in the promotion of organ donation," Rabbi Blanchard explains. "I have a donor card I always carry with me. On the back it gives you two choices regarding when it's okay to harvest your organs: one option is, once there's the cessation of autonomous breathing (brain stem death); the other is, once there's heart-death. All of us in HOD have checked the 'brain stem death' box. People all across the spectrum of Judaism are pushing Jews to get on board with organ donation, because it saves lives. You understand: this is not for purposes of research; this is to save lives. There *are* Jews, I think, who would give organs for purposes of research, but probably not Orthodox Jews."

Jewish law requires that the command to save lives be balanced with the duty to preserve one's own life and health, a Conservative ethicist points out. Blood donation is almost obligatory (health permitting). Bone-marrow donation is much harder on the donor; so, while it is praiseworthy, most rabbis would put it in a different category from blood donation. For the riskier organ donations to be acceptable under Jewish law, the likelihood of a good outcome for the recipient must far outweigh the risk to the donor's own health.

"If you go back and read in the codes of Jewish law," says a Jewish chaplain in Michigan, "you'll find that you are not allowed to desecrate the body, nor are you allowed to sell the organs. You have to explain organ donation to people in a way that helps them understand that you are not disfiguring the body; you are just taking that organ, and you're going to help somebody." Indeed, an Orthodox medical ethicist concurs, harvesting an organ *does not* desecrate a body. Moreover, he stresses, ritual concerns are always trumped by life-saving acts. A single individual might have the great honor of saving many lives, since the heart, lungs, liver, kidneys, pancreas, small intestines, corneas, and even the skin can be passed on to others.

"Organ donation is wonderful," a Michigan rabbi concludes. "We have to educate the public that this person's life goes on when his or her organs are received by someone else." Yet, even though his chaplaincy training has taught him to ask families to consider organ donation, he is reluctant to do so. "On *Yom Kippur,* I will have to atone for this!" he says.

"We encourage our fellow Muslims to give to the organ bank," a New York chaplain explains, "because we think that helps humankind. And that's what we want human beings to do: to help humankind." In fact, says a prominent New York imam, donating an organ is "an ongoing charity." He points to decisions by highly respected Islamic legal scholars in support of the permissibility of organ donation, even by a living person. While all precautions should be taken, if the donor dies in the process of organ transfer, he or she will be honored as a martyr for having died in an effort to save a life. "I am an organ donor," says a critical-care nurse—a Shi'ah Muslim. "My family cannot make this decision for me. I have to say what I want donated, and how. I have to settle it between me and God."

"As Sikhs, one of the most important things we are to do is to spend our life internalizing, consciously remembering God in everything we do," a Michigan attorney says. "Another is from the standpoint of *seva*, which is service to God's creation. The body is basically a house for our soul. Essentially, it is a house for God, because we believe God resides within each of us. So while we are on this earth we are supposed to be using the body for God's purposes. Our holy book says that if you use the body to serve God's creation, then you will realize God inside of you."

"On the other hand," she continues, "the body is temporary, and eventually it will deteriorate. Our soul will pass on, but our body will combine itself with the dust. It will become one with the earth. When someone dies, we cremate the body. We really don't have any further purpose for it. So we believe that that would be a true service to humanity to donate organs that are no longer useful to you in death to someone who needs to live onward, so they too can use their life for a good purpose. It is an important thing to see organ donation as *seva*—as service. It is also important to see the body as temporary: if we don't have a use for it and if someone else can use it, then donating it is what we are created for."

A Zoroastrianism professor agrees: the organ will simply decompose, so if it can be of any use to someone else, donating it flows naturally from the general Zoroastrian notion that each of us should provide humanity the maximum assistance we can. "I have spoken to a number of our priests about this," a medical student says, "and many say that Zoroastrianism supports whatever is best for the person." Indeed, says one priest: "I myself have signed up for organ donation. I think this way: when we die, we are supposed to dispose of our body, and give it over to nature or to vultures, or whatever; so it is the best practice nowadays, instead of placing it on the Tower of Silence, to donate the whole body to research. If they can use my whole body, that's the best way to meet our religious principles."

Receiving an organ
In conversations about religion and organ transplantation, a great deal is said about whether it is acceptable to *donate* organs but much less about whether it is all right to *receive* them. For Jews, "that is because the assumption is that anything that can be done to preserve life should be done," an Orthodox educator explains. "In fact, I think the recent extra push in favor of organ donation is coming from those Jews who are uncomfortable with being part of a community who will accept organs from others, but who won't give organs."

Allowing the implanting of animal parts into a human being raises related concerns. For example, does this constitute "consuming" an animal part? That is, how does this medical practice relate to our religion's dietary rules? For example, notes Professor Deepak Sarma, "Many Hindus are vegetarians. So, do we accept bowels from pigs?" Furthermore, he points out, some will ask, "If you have an organ from somebody else, does that mean you are going to have their *karma*? It's a fantastic question: What happens to the *karma*? Does it go with the organ?" Some ancient Hindu stories seem to offer an answer, he points out. For example, there are stories in which people receive a body part, and as a result take on (or share) the *karma* of the donor: "They wear the eye of an animal, so they are seeing things as an animal."

Medical use of animal parts is quite allowable under Jewish law, a Conservative ethicist argues, and the animal from which these parts were taken need not be kosher. They can even be taken from a pig! Receiving an implant, a graft, or a transplant is not "eating," he explains, so dietary laws do not obtain; and even if it were, the obligation to save human life trumps the rules of eating. By the same logic, a Jewish vegetarian ought to accept a medical procedure making use of an animal part if it is the best option for a good outcome.

Some Muslims condone receiving organs, but not receipt of implants made of pig products. "Just because you are Jewish or Muslim does not necessarily mean that you hold a particularly extreme or orthodox point of view," a Muslim osteopath reminds us. "Take the case of heart-valve replacement. Many of the replacement valves we use are porcine. One could make the case that if this saves a life potentially, it should be okay. But there are individuals, Jewish or Muslim, who would abhor having a valve from a pig in their heart, even though it would save their life. It really depends on the individual. I think physicians have learned—the hard way, sometimes—to handle each case on an individual basis."

The Qur'an states that we are powerless to extend our life or hasten our death. But, he stresses, God gave humanity the knowledge and ability to perform organ transplants, and wants that knowledge put to good use. The topic is now discussed more openly in the mosque than would have been the case a decade ago. A Detroit imam agrees: "There is nothing wrong with using the advancements that God gives us; just use it for good, not for evil." In fact, he says, "One of our imams received a liver transplant. It was some time ago, too. He's doing fine." Indeed, says a chaplain: "We Muslims do receive organ transplants; we give and we take."

Would Jains be comfortable receiving an organ? "One of Jainism's principles is to sustain life," says a Chicago biochemist. "That was the main goal behind arranging for a kidney transplant for my brother. I was one of the potential donors." In the end, her brother received a kidney from someone who had died in an accident. "To me, the idea is to do the least harm possible," says her sister, a physician. "So, the kidney our brother received came from a little boy who had a fatal accident. It was the decision of the family and the surgeon to use the organ to help sustain and enhance another life. So in that aspect, it fits in with Jain principles."

"I would add," says a Jain internist, "that when we receive a vital organ, someone gave up life. We would be aware that a person died an untimely death. This has to do with compassion, which is an important aspect of Jainism."

"My personal opinion," says a Sikh educator, "is that receiving an organ would be fine for most American Sikhs. Most of us don't have issues with most medical procedures. Most people wouldn't think of it any more or any less than any other operation."

"I think many Sikhs are not that keen on organ-receiving," an intensive-care nurse counters. "It all depends on the individual. I also think that when a younger person needs an organ transplant, then everybody's okay. Especially with a kidney, they are. It can come from a live donor—usually a family member—and it's okay."

For Buddhists, says Chaplain Zuniga, the issues around organ reception are similar to those regarding donation, and can be resolved by similar logic. "Again, in Buddhism, we're all interconnected. There's no 'you,' there's no 'me'; there's no difference between you and me. Organ reception is just a natural manifestation of direct realization of the practice of 'no-self.' I can't see that in any way but 'good *karma*.' Receiving an organ is also an incredible gift."

"Twice I have received cornea transplants," says a Zoroastrian priest. "According to our religion, whichever way you can help Ahura Mazda by being more proficient and healthy yourself is good. Health is also regarded as a spiritual thing. If you don't have good health, you cannot work for *frashokereti* [renovation]. So, you should try anything that will increase your goodness. There is no contradiction between organ transplantation and Zoroastrianism."

In spite of overall reluctance among American Indians, "there are people in our community who have had kidney transplants," a Mohawk chief admits. "They don't really like to do it, but some have had to do it." Others, however, have no problem with the notion of transplants, says a Keetoowah writer. "Indian people don't have a static culture. It grows. I know Indian people who have been saved by transplants. I also know Indian people who have had organ transplants and never felt right about it. So it's an individual thing. I think there are some tribes that would not allow it, traditionally. There might be individuals in those tribes who would want it, but they would probably not be following the traditions anymore anyway."

In fact, a study by Johns Hopkins University confirms that, due to the rise of Type II diabetes and kidney disease in their communities, America's First Peoples have a very high need for organ transplants, yet many are reluctant to become donors because of their belief that this will cause their spirits to remain restless after the death of the body. Advances in screening are making it easier to match donors to recipients within a tribe. This, along with targeted health education, may help overcome some of this reluctance, as will making such medical procedures affordable to the Native communities.

Allowing Natural Death

"For two years I directed a palliative care program," a Zen monk explains, "and yes, doctors, patients, families can cling to life in a way that is unskillful (as we Buddhists would put it), or in a way that causes suffering. We can cling to life in ways that are unhelpful. You see that all the time. It's a huge issue in hospitals. The one commonality of human existence that every religion would agree with is that we're mortal beings. That's the one commonality of human existence, across time, across culture, across gender, across religion. We are all mortal beings."

As we have heard from time to time in this chapter's discussion, sometimes patients and their families conclude that the most compassionate choice is an order of "Allow Natural Death" (AND, as opposed to DNR—"Do Not Resuscitate"). It is one thing to make this decision when the patient is an elderly parent; it is quite another when the patient is your child. For example, on May 20, 2005, twelve-year-old Buddhist Maya Hubner was diagnosed with acute lymphoblastic leukemia. The cancer was virulent, the treatment intense, and the complications many. Just short of a year later, her father explains, "we had the very unpleasant task of telling our daughter that she was not going to be able to survive her disease; and the very next day, we had to tell her two younger siblings. This was, needless to say, the low point of our experience."

If Maya could have been brought into remission, and if a donor match could be found, her parents were going to pursue a bone-marrow transplant. But even the most aggressive chemotherapy possible did not arrest Maya's leukemia. Her father came to the certainty that a transplant attempt was not likely to work, other experimental therapies were too risky, and to try either approach might even be cruel. "I knew at that point how glorious it would be to have her at home," her father recalls. And Maya agreed. "When told we could not find a cure for her leukemia, Maya asked, 'What does that mean?' Her doctor said, 'Honey, it means that you cannot survive your disease.' Maya said, 'Does it mean I'm going to die?' And her doctor said, 'Yes, you're going to die; but we don't know *when* you're going to die.' That became an important theme for us, and we talked pretty openly about death: none of us know when we're going to die."

"But what resulted then," Maya's father continues, "was a final seven—almost eight—weeks under hospice care, and she got to live a fairly normal life. The Broviac—the catheter device that was in her side, so they could access the main artery with medicines and chemotherapy—was removed. She got to go into a swimming pool. She got to be at home." She was also able to travel from Austin to San Diego, compliments of the Make-A-Wish Foundation, where she swam with the dolphins. In her father's most treasured photo of that trip, just one month before her death, Maya is holding a rose. She looks happy, even *healthy,* and beautifully serene.

How do the religions of our neighbors help them when death does arrive? It is to that we now turn.

CHAPTER FOUR

Transition

"THE DYING PROCESS is transitional," an Orthodox rabbi asserts. "Yes, there are cases where it is abrupt. But often, the process begins with a person who has been ill for a while. There comes a point when you realize that the doctor is not going to make this person better. That's not going to happen. We continue to pray for the person, but we understand that there is going to be a transition here." This chapter is about how various religions mark that transition.

When Death Is Imminent

"In the exposure I have had to people who are dying," reflects a young Zoroastrian physician, "the basic thing I see is the importance of the prayers. And when I speak of Zoroastrian prayers, I don't necessarily mean our ritual *kusthi* prayers, where we tie and untie the waistcord. I mean any prayer, really. When you're moving on, the reassurance and strength that comes with the prayers seems really important. Even people who were not observant—ever—now seem to need this comfort. That is not limited to the Zoroastrian community."

A rabbi agrees. "In Jewish tradition, when a person is approaching that moment of death, you would have somebody there reciting psalms."

"Sikhs believe that saying prayers while the soul is leaving will help that soul get to God faster," says an intensive-care nurse. "In the hospital, when there a code situation, often the staff asks the family to leave the room. But the Sikh family will want to be there when the death is declared, or when they feel that the soul is leaving. I think it can be very important to just let them be at the periphery—present, but where they won't interfere with the staff."

"Our prayers are in song form," says a Hindu Midwesterner. "My aunt was in a coma for quite a while before she died last September, and during that period, my relatives and I thought it might help to play devotional music to her. We played some of her favorites—especially a very nice song in praise of Lord Ganesha. Ganesha, of course, is the Remover of Obstructions. Ganesha didn't remove any obstructions: at last, she passed away. Or, one might say, Ganesha *did* remove obstructions and allowed her to die."

"When a Muslim is about to transition—and I prefer to say 'transition' rather than 'die'—now the family work begins," a Muslim critical-care nurse explains. "The person's bed should be turned to face Mecca, and the family needs to talk to the soul, to make sure the soul is comforted. For most people, it may be a cultural obligation to be present, but for Muslims, it is a religious obligation, and there is great reward. Angels actually follow you and stay with you."

"My grandmother had cancer, and wanted to die a natural death," a Muslim journalist relates. "About a week before she died, the doctors stopped most of the medications, and the family moved her back to her house. Family and friends started coming from all over. Throughout that week, there were always people in the room who would read Qur'an for her. Mostly, they read *Surah Ya Sin* (Chapter 36, which is known as the heart of the Qur'an) and *Surat'l-Mulk* (Chapter 67, which is supposed to help intercede for the person on the Day of Judgment and for the punishment of the grave). They'd have a tape going in the background when people weren't actually reading themselves. As she passed, everybody came together and said, *La ilaha illa'Llah*, 'There is no god but God.'"

Many a Buddhist says that it is essential that a dying person's mind be well-focused. "You should keep reciting the name of the Holy Buddha, because the only thing you want is for him to take you to the Pure Land," says a Chinese-American hospital administrator, "so that you will not to have to come back to this world again. As Buddhists we accept that, when a human body is leaving this world, it's in pain. That is because we are made out of four elements: water, wind, fire, and earth. In normal, daily living, when we are well and don't have any sickness, it is because these four elements are equally balanced. When we are sick, it is because something is not balanced. When we are dying, it is because these four elements are separating. When these four elements are separating, it can affect your mind. So, even a person who practices deeply every day may need other people's help in that moment. That's why there are also groups who volunteer to go to the hospital or to the home of the person who is dying to help them to recite. They would be at the bedside, chanting the holy name of *O-mi-to-fwo*."

When a member of his Theravada Buddhist community was dealing with the final stage of cancer, the Venerable Kondanna recalls, "almost every day one of the monks visited her and chanted with her, because we knew what was going to be the end result, and we wanted her to be in the best mental state." Did the monks do the Impermanence Chant? "Not really; no. We did not talk about that," he explains. "We didn't want her to be burdened with that thought. We did the *Metta* chant—*metta* means loving-kindness."

Tibetan Buddhists say that, as a person dies, the four elements [water, wind, fire, earth] "dissolve" or "lose their strength." This is what it means to pass through the *bardos*. "As you go through this dissolution stage," one layman explains, "images of mirage, smoke, fireflies, a flickering candle appear in your subtle consciousness. Then, after those four images, you see a white light, a red light, and then a black light, and then something called clear light. By becoming familiar with this, people learn to control the death process. A strong practitioner will actually meditate on facsimiles of these images. It is said that by doing this, you may actually attain liberation or enlightenment at the death time. Then you are no longer under the sway of uncontrolled rebirth. You'll become a Buddha, a perfect being, and can return out of concern for others. Only by becoming a Buddha can you really benefit others in the most effective way. So, we try to make awareness of the death process a way for us to help others."

His Holiness the Dalai Lama stresses that, regardless of whether a person follows a spiritual path, it is important to help him or her die with serenity of mind. The best way to make sure this is possible, he says, is to create a loving, tender environment for the dying person. He calls it "tragic in the extreme" for a person to be abandoned and deprived of affection at the time of death. When someone is dying, a disciple explains, "it is good to have each of the senses reminding him or her of his or her spiritual practice. It's good to see pictures of Buddha, of the person's teacher or teachers; to smell incense, if it is allowed; to hear prayers, reminders, sacred words, pleasant words, peaceful words. For touch, we have a *mala,* a rosary. It might be good to place that in the dying person's hand. For taste, we have some ritually blessed pills made of herbs, flour, and precious metals. The point is to remind the dying person, as gently as possible, of their Buddhist practice."

"One particularly interesting thing," a Theravada student chaplain notes, "is the way that the dying person sometimes actually facilitates a special practice for the community by allowing others to be in the presence of death and to work with it. Recently, I visited a dying person whose room felt like a meditation hall. There were cushions set around. Some of his visitors were deep in sitting-meditation or other forms of practice. Not only did the community come together to do this, but the dying person and the dying person's family made the space available for this."

Many Zen practitioners mention how valuable they find the *Bardo Thodol*—the Tibetan Book of the Dead. When a member of his practice-community was at the final stage of a lengthy illness, "I read into her ear from the Tibetan Book of the Dead," a Michigan Zen instructor explains. "That eased her passage. When I finished, she died." He finished, and she let go.

Actually, says a Zen chaplain, "it's good to study the Tibetan Book of the Dead throughout your life. But especially in a hospice setting, especially if somebody is near death, it is very efficacious to read it. Often, spiritual autobiographies tend to look at how a person lived, and that's very good; but in Buddhism we say that it's also very important to look at how the person died. When you're learning how to die, you're also learning how to live. Like everything in existence, they're interconnected."

Right about the time his twelve-year-old daughter's leukemia reinvigorated itself, attorney Chris Hubner (whom we met at the end of chapter three) read a newspaper article in which Buddhist chaplain David Zuniga was quoted as saying, "Suffering is the teacher." "I just picked up the telephone, and I hunted him down! I said, 'David, I don't know you, but I've got this daughter with leukemia, and here's our story. And listen: if you know anything about suffering, I would like to talk to you.' David was in Maya's hospital room that next afternoon."

"David not only helped Maya, but he helped all of us," Mr. Hubner stresses. "As we took our descent with Maya, as news got worse and worse and worse, we'd think, How can it get worse? But it does get worse. And the suffering you're exposed to as a parent: it's just indescribable. You have to learn that it *is* suffering, and that you have to see it for what it is. As the Buddhists say, you have to sit with suffering, and let it penetrate you. Then—lo and behold—you're in those last eight weeks. We achieved a lot of *joy* out of that suffering. I am just so grateful that we sat with the suffering, rather than resisting and fighting and being in denial, and sending Maya from Austin to Houston for experimental treatments. That would not have been very effective."

One June evening, a drastically weakened thirteen-year-old Maya said to her chaplain: "The first step to becoming a Buddha is to overcome your fear of death. . . . I don't want anyone to feel sad for me. I am happy. I have led a full life." Thirty-six hours later, just thirteen months after her diagnosis, she was gone.

Once Death Has Come

The transition, even when anticipated, is not devoid of mystery. "Think of a person," says a physician—a devout Hindu. "He and I are sitting in the living room, having a conversation. Suddenly, for one reason or another, this person dies. His body is now lying on the floor. A few minutes ago, it was living; now it is dead. But it is the same body. What happened? What is the difference? What left the body? What was there which is not there now? That's the question I have!"

But there is no mystery that, when death has indeed come, something must be done with the body. Whatever the decision, serious participants in a religion community are guided by their religion's principles as they proceed. Most move directly to the funeral; for some, questions of autopsy or donation of the body to medical or scientific research must be answered first.

Autopsy
Those who have difficulty with the notion of organ donation often are opposed to performing an autopsy, for similar reasons. One imam could be speaking for adherents of many different religions when he asserts, "The deceased should be given the same dignity as when he or she was alive," and some people of faith are reluctant to see autopsy as a dignified affair. One Jain forensic dentist calls the autopsy portion of his medical-examiner training "the most horrifying experience I ever had in my life." Virtually everyone agrees, however, that the civic need to solve a crime trumps religious objections to autopsy.

Donating the body for research
When it comes to donation of the body to medical research, religious objections are fewer across the board. "We wouldn't have the technology and the medicine we have available to us

without that science," a Sikh points out. "So I think it is really important that we look at the issue from the perspective that every single one of us benefits. We take advantage of it if we go to a hospital or a doctor. Compassion is the key here."

Again, the concern is that the body be accorded dignity. Some Jewish legal interpreters condone donation of a body to a medical school only if all parts would be given a proper Jewish burial when no longer needed. "In anatomy classes, we had a lot of discussions about how we should treat this person who sacrificed their own body," a Jain physician recalls. "Every time I did an autopsy or a dissection, I would fast as penance and forgiveness from whatever persons or animals I hurt during my training. Some medical schools now accord the appropriate respect to the body before it is disposed of."

Disposing of the Body

When it comes to disposing of the remains, burial and cremation are the obvious possibilities. However, before we hear from people for whom one of these might not only may be preferred but required, we should mention a third practice characteristic of some religions.

Sky Burial
In a high-mountain habitat with little fuel and hard ground, neither cremation nor burial are practical. Therefore, in their homeland, Tibetan Buddhists could choose to offer their bodies to the vultures as a last act of generosity. The body would be taken to a special place where—reverently and ceremonially— it would be cut into small pieces (bones and all), then offered to the birds. Assuming one did indicate one's intention to undergo Sky Burial, then, a monk explains, "it would be of benefit for you in a future lifetime, and will ultimately be of benefit for others."

In India, many Zoroastrians still transport the body of a deceased family member to a traditional *dakhma,* a Tower of

Silence, where the flesh is consumed by birds of prey and the wear and tear of the elements. Once the bones are bleached, they are deposited into a chamber within the tower, where they decompose and return to the soil. This is ecological, says a Zoroastrian filmmaker. "Absolutely," a medical student agrees. "It is about giving life back to life." From a Zoroastrian point of view, she explains, burying a corpse is problematic: "You would be putting dead matter back into the ground, and that could pollute the earth." Reportedly, at least one Zoroastrian community is in the process of building a Tower of Silence in North America, but for now, American Zoroastrians make other arrangements.

Traditionally the Ojibway Indians would have laid out their dead in a high place—on a platform placed on scaffolding. A nurse in Detroit's Ojibway community would like to have done that for her recently deceased mother, but made do with burial instead.

Burial

In the Ojibway tradition, Lucy Harrison explains, "women carry the responsibility for water. All beings are related to water, but the woman is related to it more intimately. So, women conduct all water ceremonies"—which means that it falls to the women of the community to prepare a body for burial. "We wash the dead with cedar water," she continues. "When you boil cedar twigs for around an hour and a half, the water turns to the color of a red rose—really dark. Then it is ready to use for the washing. And we don't just do it once. If we have a deceased person with us for a day and a half or two, then we'll do the washing all day and all night. There are certain songs that we offer to the Creator, songs that are saved only for that time. Traditionally, we would lay the body out in a house hung with colors appropriate to that person, to where that person is headed. Colors all are symbolic. They represent different deities, and our relationship to them and to the environment."

America's various First Nations have their particular burial customs. When a Lakota dies, burial is preceded by a wake for two or three nights, says a Californian who grew up on the Pine Ridge Reservation. Whether it is performed in Christian or traditional fashion, "the burial usually happens in the afternoon," he explains, "and then we have a big feed afterward. We give the person's possessions away to the people who are there: clothing, horses, guns—whatever they owned."

Traditionally, "Mohawks would lay people out for two days where their home is," a chief explains. "Once the body is there, somebody stays there all night and all day; and usually there are several of them. They never leave the body, ever. That's why we don't like to put it in a funeral home. They close at a certain time; and then we've got to leave. For us, it's disrespectful to leave." While his community may not be entirely comfortable with using funeral homes, they have become more willing to accept embalming, and to wait several days to bury, in order to give family members of the deceased a chance to travel home.

"When somebody dies in a clan, the other members of that clan are said to be in mourning," he notes. They are not permitted to touch the dead, or do the grave-digging. That is the task of some other clan within the Mohawk Nation. "The immediate family aren't supposed to touch the body or do anything. They are just supposed to cry."

There will be lots of food at a Mohawk funeral, he says. "We don't bury the dead if there's not food there; the older food, like beans and corn, corn silks, cornbread; the real ancient food, like raspberries, blueberries; the real, real food—that's the most powerful. You try to eat as much as you can, but you don't have to gorge yourself." The point, he says, is that "the more you eat, the more you're feeding the dead; but you don't have to overdo it. You have to be reasonable. You eat a little more than you normally eat, because you're feeding the dead. We have a lot of relatives, so we try to eat as much as we can, to honor them. When it's over, you put the leftover food back on the ground, in the field somewhere. You don't want your dog or your cat to eat it. They're domesticated animals. You want the animal that's free to eat it, because the soul is free from the world. That's why you want the bird that's not in a cage, the cat that's not in a cage, the dog that's not in a cage. The wolf, or coyote, or deer, or whatever—that's the one. Once the food goes back to nature, it goes back to God."

Traditionally, the Cherokee community would have kept the body of the deceased in their home for four days, usually in a pine box. "We do it quicker these days," healer Dawi Wistona explains. "The belief is that the Life Force of that person hangs around the body for seven days. You would do ceremony for that time, to protect that Life Force. Otherwise, it could actually be stolen by somebody who knows how to use it for nefarious purposes. The body is washed. Some people still paint the face black and red. In the old days, they would tie a cloth around the head—white cloth—to keep the jaw from dropping. That's usually not done anymore. Usually, the body is dressed in ceremonial clothing. Usually there would be cedar in the casket—cedar, and tobacco, and maybe a few personal things that they might want buried with them. In most funeral ceremonies, there is a death song that is sung. Most of the ceremony is for the survivors. The person has gone on. Assuming they don't have any overwhelming reason to stay, we believe that they go naturally to where they are supposed to go: to the Darkening Land.

"The body should not be left alone," says Keetoowah author Yvonne Wakim Dennis. "Family or friends stay with it." Nowadays, this can create some humorous situations, she explains, "because we are living in a non-Cherokee world." For example, when an Ojibway friend died recently in a Manhattan hospital, Yvonne and several other friends wanted to keep vigil with the body for twenty-four hours. "The body was in a drawer in a cold-storage room, and the staff wouldn't let us stay in there. But we're very adaptable people; we've had to be. So after staying with the body as long as we were allowed, we went to the quiet hospital chapel to reminisce and comfort the family. After the body was transported to a funeral home, the eight of us all went to a little park nearby. People were all around—it's a public park. My friend Rosie, an Apache pipe carrier, said, 'We're going to pray now, but don't worry; we'll be invisible.' So we were invisible. We said prayers of thanksgiving for our friend's life, and prayed that there would be people around to help the grieving. People were walking around us—a group of Indians sitting in a circle, smoking a pipe. That's not something you see in a public park every day. But they *did* ignore us."

"Most of the Native people I know want to be cremated," Yvonne continues, "because they don't want to be dug up a hundred years from now and probed and studied in the way our ancestors have been treated. When I die, I want to be cremated. I just want a simple cardboard box that's not going to pollute too much when it's burned. I don't want money wasted on a casket when people are starving." However, she says, burial is more traditional for Cherokees than cremation. "Growing up, my Indian family used to say, 'You can't be buried without all your parts.' So when I had my wisdom teeth removed, I saved them. When I first got married, my husband was going through some boxes and found my four wisdom teeth. I said, 'You've got to leave them there in case I die. I've got to be buried with them!' But again, I know Cherokee people who don't think this way. Many of them are Christians, while others have beliefs mixed with Christianity or with customs from other tribes."

When someone dies in the Jewish community, "it is traditional to spill a little bit of water to indicate the body's passing, that the soul has passed," says an Orthodox rabbi. It is also customary to have someone called a *shomer* or *shomera*—a guard—who sits by the body and recites psalms. Here again is another religion-community that insists that the body is not to be left alone. And, a Conservative chaplain stresses, "the body should not be moved more than absolutely necessary, out of respect for the dead. Some hospitals want to move the body into the morgue pretty quickly, which means you can't be next to the body. At the hospital I served, they were really great about letting the deceased person stay in the room as long as possible. They had a whole protocol about care of observant Jews who have died and how to care for people who have died on *Shabbat* specifically. In situations where they had to take the person down to the morgue, they would allow a *shomer* or *shomera* to sit outside the morgue. And it was just understood that this was the best we could do under the circumstances. But that was hard."

What about the ritual washing and shrouding of the body? "This is one of those areas where there isn't too much law, but a great deal of custom," an Orthodox educator explains. "When someone dies, a *chevra khadisha*—a holy fellowship group—gets together. They wash the body. If the deceased is a man, they're men; if it's a woman, they're women." However, a person whose clothing became soaked in his or her blood when dying is not washed, because blood is holy. The body is wrapped in a *kittel*, a simple white shroud. "There are elaborate rituals as to how all of this is done," she continues. "Again, the sense of the dignity of the body is incredibly important, and very central to that ceremony."

Jews don't hold a wake, an Orthodox rabbi emphasizes. If there is no Jewish funeral home at hand, "there are non-Jewish funeral homes with somebody on staff who knows our customs. The funeral itself will take place as quickly as possible, unless you have to wait for people to come from out of town. You want to show respect for the dead, so if there's family coming from out of town, we'll wait." Most Jewish funerals take place at a funeral home or "funeral chapel" rather than a synagogue. "We have had a funeral in the sanctuary only once," says the cantor of a Reform synagogue in New Jersey. "It was for a gentleman who had been the president of our congregation for over twenty-five years. The congregation wanted to honor him; and it was entirely appropriate that we hold his memorial service in the sanctuary."

In the more traditional Jewish circles, the casket is a very plain, unadorned pine box. Whatever the denomination, "Don't expect an open coffin at a Jewish funeral," says a Conservative rabbi, "because the guiding principle is to remember that person as they were with you. An open coffin is very jarring to a Jewish person." Rabbi Tzvi Blanchard concurs. "What I usually say to people who say 'I want to see him one last time,' is 'You *can't* see him one last time. What you see is not the person. These are the remains.'"

Think of it this way, Rabbi Blanchard suggests: "You have a college roommate. All of a sudden he has an enormous study opportunity, but he has to be there in forty-eight hours. The only way for him to do it is to just pack a suitcase and go. He has left lots of stuff in the dorm room. So he says, 'Look. Would you just do me a favor? Would you take responsibility for packing these things up and sending them back to my parents? Here's the address.' It's the same thing: in death, people have no choice; they have to go. They themselves can't do anything with the body. So they say: 'These are my remains. Would you please see to them after I'm gone?' And it is our privilege to do that for them."

The casket is closed, "but you very much feel the presence of the person," a Talmud scholar notes. "That is very significant. The idea is that you have come to pay honor to the person who has passed. Therefore, the body is there."

"At the funeral, there is this ritual activity called *kriav* [tearing], which is done by the family of the deceased," an Orthodox rabbi explains. "It's been called a symbolic rending of the heart. For your parents, you never completely sew it up again." Traditional Jews will tear their actual garment right down the side. However, some Jews (particularly in the Reform Movement) tear a black ribbon which they then pin to their lapel. "Even some Modern Orthodox rip a ribbon," a Reconstructionist rabbi notes. "I am a Liberal Jew, but when someone in my family dies, I am going to want to rip my clothing (rather than just wear a torn ribbon) because I think it is *such* a powerful symbol."

"If you go to a Jewish funeral," notes a Conservative rabbi, "you'd better get there on time. A Jewish funeral is punctual and very brief." No matter which stream of Judaism, it will include psalms. "I usually sing Psalm 16," says a Reform cantor; "then, after I do a short reading, I have the people join me in reading Psalm 23 in English." There may be other readings from scripture, and then the eulogy will be given. "Eulogizing used to be an art form," says one Orthodox rabbi. Traditionally, this would be the rabbi's task, but rabbis often must officiate at funerals for people who are not affiliated with their congregation. "In that case," says a Reform rabbi, "I will ask a family member or friend; it will be more personal." Finally, *El Molei Rachamim,* the traditional prayer recalling all who have gone before, is often said or chanted. "As the family and I follow the casket out of the funeral chapel," a Reform cantor says, "I chant psalms. Then we go directly to the graveside."

"We *bury;* we don't cremate," an Orthodox rabbi explains. "It's interesting. Very few Jews, whatever their affiliation, will select cremation." In fact, most rabbis will not officiate at a funeral if the body has been cremated, although some Reform rabbis will. "The body is part of who we are," he continues, "and there is a faith, somehow, in the restoration of the body—that it lasts somehow. It's not a matter of logic alone; it's a matter of images."

The casket will be carried to graveside by pallbearers, then it will be placed in the ground. At the graveside ceremony, a rabbi may lead prayers of mourning for the dead. Psalms 23 and 90 (which speak of comfort), and *El Molei Rachamim* may be recited. "Especially for family members, there is a really strong sense of wanting to participate in the burial," says Devorah Zlochower, "even though at the same time it is very difficult. There is a sense that seeing to a proper burial is the last favor you are doing for this person. The term we use in Hebrew for anything associated with taking care of someone who is dead is *chesed shel emet*—a kindness of truth, or a truthful kindness. You are doing a kindness for someone who is not in the position to pay you back. That is considered to be a really unselfish, altruistic act."

Shovels will be available, and the immediate family and friends take turns in shoveling the dirt into the grave—traditionally, until the grave is completely covered, she notes. "The gravediggers are not the ones who do the burial; the family does the burial. The custom is also to use the shovel 'backwards'—at least when you start off. Instead of holding the shovel the way you would normally, you pick up the dirt with the *back* of the shovel. It is meant to show our reluctance to get this done with fast. Obviously, it's going to be more laborious to do it this way and that's fine, because you are saying goodbye to this person." This is more a matter of custom than law, a rabbi suggests; there is more than one right way to accomplish this task.

"As far as Jewish law is concerned," Ms. Zlochower continues, "the act of burying someone is a good thing. For example, according to Jewish law, priests are not to become ritually defiled by contact with a dead body. But if a priest—even the high priest—is walking on the way and sees a person who has not been buried, he is *required* to defile himself and make sure that person has been buried—that *mitzvah* is of such high magnitude."

Participating physically in the burial of a loved one can be cathartic. "We allow anyone to take part who wants to—not just the family," a Reform cantor says, but in her congregation, each person puts in just a shovelful. A Conservative rabbi says he insists that the family fill in the grave, because it is such an important act symbolically.

Once the shoveling is accomplished, it is time for the family to recite the Mourner's *Kaddish*. This prayer is in Aramaic, and does not mention death. Rather, it speaks of the meaning of life, of immortality, redemption, community, and peace.

"After the person has been buried, people will line up in two rows," an Orthodox rabbi explains. "The mourners will walk between them, and people will say this formula that indicates that they should be comforted." A Reform rabbi maintains this custom, because "sometimes people have real difficulty leaving and letting go. As difficult as it is, it is important for them to move on to the next step of their mourning." For Orthodox, offering condolences to the family is not appropriate before this moment; Reform Jews may have done so already.

In Orthodox circles, a Talmud scholar explains, legal strictures apply to those who are descended from *Kohanim*, the priestly families who served the ancient temple in Jerusalem. "They will attend burials only of close family members—parents, children, siblings—but will not generally go to cemeteries, and will not be in the room where a body is present. So if you go to a traditional Jewish funeral you will see, outside the synagogue or outside the funeral home, a bunch of men standing there. They are all *Kohanim;* they are not going inside—unless the deceased is immediate family."

"Death brings a time of meditation and sorrow to all of us," a Shi'ah imam explains. "It is a time when we all reflect upon the life hereafter. Therefore, in Islam, there are instructions given to Muslims about how the dead person should be handled. One of the most important things that we have to be concerned with is that the deceased has to be handled with so much dignity and respect."

Interestingly, even in American cities with dense Muslim populations, there are very few Islamic funeral homes. Instead, Muslim communities tend to seek out a local funeral home that is willing to accommodate Islamic practices around preparation of the body for burial. A Connecticut educator describes a situation that is common around the country: "The imam goes to one of the funeral homes with which his mosque has an agreement. The funeral director opens the doors, we bring the body from the hospital, and then we are left alone to do our rituals. Each funeral home develops a relationship with a particular mosque."

"We have trained a committee of about fifteen people to do the washing," explains a member of Greater Detroit's large Shi'ah community. "We work as teams: one team leader plus two team players. We do a pre-washing with vegetable-based soap and water. Then the body is rinsed three times: first, with water into which we have stirred *sidr,* a powder that comes from the lote tree; then, with a solution of camphor and water. Finally, the body is rinsed lightly with plain water, so that the *sidr* and camphor (which are natural antibacterial agents) will not be removed completely. The body lies face up the whole time. We wash the head first; then, the right side (front, then back) from shoulder to toes; then the left side in the same way. We dry the body in the same way. As we work, we play a tape of the Qur'an. We refrain from small talk. Shi'ah believe that the deceased is conscious of what we're doing. The soul is going through a traumatic change. If we say anything at all, it is to express our understanding to the soul—that we know what it is going through."

"A female Muslim washes a female, and the male washes the male," explains a Sunni imam in New York. "But either can wash the children under the age of puberty. And also, the husband has the right to wash his wife, and the wife has a right to wash her husband. We try to have at least two or three people do it. We don't want too many people in there. It can cause a lot of confusion. Now there have been times when I have had to do it myself, alone."

If a corpse is in really bad condition, water is not used, a Shi'ah businessman clarifies. And, "if we don't have the whole body, we wash what we have. I have picked up amputated limbs from the hospital and have washed them for burial. I will wash miscarried fetuses—some not even as long as my little finger. I can't do the full procedure because they are too tiny, but we still treat them with respect." Not only did nurse Najah Bazzy, a

Shi'ah Muslim, convince her Michigan hospital to stop discarding miscarried fetuses, she also founded Plots for Tots, a program that assists any family who cannot afford funeral arrangements for their deceased infant or fetus.

Sunni and Shi'ah methods of preparing a body for burial differ somewhat, notes Abdullah Antepli, associate director of Hartford Seminary's Islamic Chaplaincy Program. "Regardless, the basic thing is to wash the complete body. That is the minimum. Essentially, it is the same complete ritual body-washing we do for a number of reasons while we are alive. It is called *ghusl*. The body should be washed by a Muslim while certain prayers and supplications are made. We ask for forgiveness for the deceased person; we seek God's welcome for him or her with God's mercy and blessings, and to make her journey from the grave to the Day of Judgment easy. Other than completely washing the body three times, the other details are pretty much determined by the culture."

"After the religious washing will be a shrouding, which is several layers of white cloth—for purity, very simple—as a symbol that everybody is equal in God's eyes," explains a mortician who has served dozens of Muslim families. "We use five pieces for a woman, three pieces for a man, and one for a child." His funeral home has shrouding cloth ready at all times. However, the family might opt to provide their own. Some Muslims wish to be buried in the white cloth they wore on *Hajj*.

"Preparing the body for burial, and being in prayerfulness as you do it, is a ritual that reinforces the teaching that a Muslim should be mindful of death," says a Sunni research librarian. "You should know that death could come at any moment, so we should be prepared. Adult Muslims should have made a will. We should have the things necessary for washing the body on hand. We should have our burial shroud available. I don't think most of us have done these things." Too often in the American context, she says, family members no longer participate in the washing. "When you live in a twenty-first-century, super-modern, urban environment, it is easy to become disconnected from this age-old ritual that reinforces such a significant part of Islamic theology."

"Right after shrouding will be casketing," says the owner of a Detroit funeral home. He uses biodegradable caskets, either wood or cardboard, since Michigan law requires that the body must be placed in a container. "Eventually, the body will be in touch with the earth one more time. The Muslim belief is that the human has been created from this dirt, and to the dirt will go back; and from this dirt we'll come again at the resurrection. We don't embalm. We use herbs and spices and strong odors—pleasant ones to overcome the smell of death. Anything like perfume can be used, as long as it does not have an alcohol base, because alcohol is forbidden."

"After the preparations are done," says a Dearborn resident, "the deceased is taken to a mosque or a religious center, although that is not mandatory. Simply because people would like to have a last look or to pay respect, the body is brought to an Islamic Center. After being given a eulogy by the imam, the family and friends join the imam in performing the *janaazah,* a special prayer over the body of the deceased. We ask God to forgive this person, and if he is a good person, to reward him. After that, the person is taken to the cemetery."

"In the Islamic faith, the grave has to be dug in a certain way," a funeral director notes. "Muslims place the deceased in the grave on their right shoulder, with the eye looking toward Mecca, waiting for the resurrection." The region around Detroit has a number of Islamic cemeteries. "We'd like to have the burial as soon as possible after death," says a Detroit imam. "Generally, it's the next day—or at least within two days. That's the general rule. If a person is to be rushed on to heaven because they've done good, you want them rushed on to heaven! If a person has done evil, you want him rushed to hell! The Prophet said we should rush the deceased to the grave. Sometimes, we bury them in the same day." However, burying quickly is a challenge in the American context, says a Bronx activist: "It is hard to get bodies released on the same day as death."

"Muslims are urged to carry the coffin on their shoulders, and go with the deceased to the cemetery," an imam explains. "Probably this is to remind us to see the destiny of each person, so we will not feel so arrogant and selfish. No matter how much you have accumulated in this life, you put it all back. All you take with you is your good deeds and bad deeds; and you will be held accountable for all of your deeds. Basically that is the funeral in Islam. In addition, there are some local, cultural traditions that involve people donating money to the poor on the soul of the deceased, offering poor people some food, meals to the needy, the less privileged."

When, in March 2007, a Bronx house fire killed ten African immigrants (nine of them children), Nurah Ammat'ullah was deployed by New York Disaster Chaplaincy Services to care for the survivors, and to assist during the funeral—for which thousands turned out. The crowd was several blocks deep in all directions. The streets were covered with blue plastic so Muslims could perform their midday *salat* just prior to the funeral itself. But many found themselves side by side with non-Muslims as they did so. "I had to do some educating around that," Chaplain Ammat'ullah recalls. "I had to make it clear to my Muslim sisters and brothers that it is okay for non-Muslims to participate in the *janaazah,* to do more than just be there. The *janaazah* does not entail all of the motions we do when we make *salat.* There is no prostration. Basically, you stand and you offer supplication on behalf of the dead. Really, anyone *can* do that, but some in the Muslim community were uncertain as to whether non-Muslims *should* be next to Muslims in the prayer lines. I was able to smooth out the situation."

"We can have a religious service for the deceased without the body being present," a Muslim hospital chaplain notes. "I think that's important. It's called *janaazah prayer in absentia.* It's the regular prayer for the deceased, as though the person was right there; and it's still accepted in al-Islam. That brings a lot of closure to the family. In Islam, we can have closure, because the Qur'an permits this."

For members of the Bahá'í Faith, "Bahá'u'lláh defines death as the separation of the soul from the body," a physician explains. "The soul then is progressing on into the next world. The organic thing, the body, is in a process of decomposition. Bahá'ís are encouraged to follow the Bahá'í law whenever possible. There are two major prohibitions pertaining to the question of burial and the condition of the body: one is against cremation; the other is against embalming. There are specific writings about that."

Indeed, in 1971, the Bahá'í Faith's Universal House of Justice explained that since the human body forms gradually, it must also be allowed to decompose gradually. "This is according to the real and natural order and Divine Law," the ruling declares. "If it had been better for it to be burned after death, in its very creation it would have been so planned that the body would automatically become ignited after death, be consumed and turned into ashes." Instead, God has provided a process by which the body "may gradually combine and mix with other elements, thus going through stages until it arrives in the vegetable kingdom, there turning into plants and flowers, developing into trees of the highest paradise, becoming perfumed and attaining the beauty of color."

Cremation interferes with these transformations. "If civil law, however, requires embalming or cremation," notes a cancer specialist, "this invokes another principle of the Bahá'í Faith, which is to be the well-wishers of those in authority, and to be obedient to a duly constituted government and to the laws of the land. Under those conditions, Bahá'ís may be embalmed or cremated."

"Bahá'í laws are very prescriptive about how burial is to take place," a Bahá'í businesswoman points out. "The body is to be washed, then wrapped in silk cloth if possible; there are some other elements. We need to consider various relatives and friends who may not be accustomed to the lack of embalming. The deceased is to be buried immediately; and the body of the deceased is not to be transported more than one hour's distance from where he or she died to this world. That particular Bahá'í law is not strictly enforced at this time, but that *is* the law in Bahá'í Faith."

The Bahá'í Faith may be prescriptive, but it has no professional clergy nor set ritual for its observances or functions, one member reminds us. "A funeral is put together by the family, or by the community. However, there is a prayer for the dead which was revealed to us by Bahá'u'lláh," he notes. "It is the only prayer that is said congregationally. The purpose of the service, of the washing of the body, the use of shrouds—all of these have the dual purpose of memorializing and commemorating the separation of the soul and the body, but also of giving comfort to the family in their hour of grief."

Unlike the Bahá'í Faith, Taoism, like Christianity, has many different sects. As a *Qigong* master points out, "Episcopalians do not do what the Catholics do; Catholics do not do what the Baptists do. So it is with us." The exact details of funeral rituals may differ between various expressions of Taoism; there may be differences between the way rituals are performed in America and the way they are done in China—and with these differences come occasional arguments as to whose version is most authentic. Furthermore, the line between Taoist and Buddhist customs may not be clear-cut. A memorial service for the deceased will be officiated by a spiritual teacher. Since Taoist priests are hard to find in America, a family might call in a Buddhist monk or nun. Some families try to cover all bases, he says. "A Christian clergyperson will speak, the Buddhist monk or nun will chant, and the Taoist will do the ritual." The family of the departed may wear sackcloth garments to the funeral. "You go in very bad clothing. You are mourning. You are not interested in your appearance to other people."

Taoists do not believe in embalming or cremation. Traditionally, at the memorial service, the family circles the open casket three times, chanting. The spouse and son honor him with bowing and incense, an educator says; the daughters and grandchildren do the same. "Each generation pays respect," notes Sat Chuen Hon. The coffin is then closed and placed in the hearse. The eldest son rides with the coffin. "He will hold a large incense stick. He'll hold it out the window. In case the spirit of the deceased gets lost, the incense will guide him. You call the name of the deceased every five minutes to remind him."

When his father died, Master Hon explains, "before we drove to the cemetery, we took one last circle around my father's normal daily path, with the hearse. We got to see what he did each day. We passed the place where he bought his groceries, where he shopped for clothes, where he would see his friends. It was very nice. Then we continued to the cemetery in New Jersey, with my brother calling out to help him, to make sure he did not get lost."

Master Hon's father was to be buried in a New Jersey cemetery. That was a problem, he notes, "because we had to cross the Hudson River to get there, and it is believed that the spirit cannot cross water. To cross the water, you have to bribe the water! You throw some paper money out the window. That's the toll that will allow the deceased's spirit to cross over. Then you bring him to the cemetery." A Taoist master will have picked a gravesite. "That is called burial *feng shui,* burial geomancy," he explains. Some cemeteries, like National Memorial Park in Virginia, have *feng shui* consultants. "The site should be sunny, but not too much; it should not be too wet. Choosing the right plot is a critical component of traditional Taoist burial and memorial service." It should be done with the same care one would exercise in buying a home in which a family would expect to live for a lifetime, he stresses. "It is no different." Because of his priestly training, Master Hon was the member of his family singled out for the honor of choosing his father's burial plot.

Having reached the cemetery, "you circle the gravesite three times," he continues. The coffin is put to rest and then the family actually has a picnic in the cemetery, right at the gravesite. "At a Chinese funeral, people wail and chant; they really let go. And when you are finished with it, you have a big feast!" At his father's graveside meal, the menu included "eggs, wine, meat dishes—a whole chicken, suckling pigs, rice, all the favorite dishes my father liked. We got to taste what he liked to eat."

When we speak of "Taoist practice," Sat Hon stresses, we should make a distinction between its householder and monastic forms. "I myself am a householder, in a very classical transmission. I am in the twenty-first generation of the Dragon Gate Household." In America's Chinatowns, he explains, we'll find little storefront Taoist temples. They are run by householder practitioners, he says. Such a temple functions like a community center. Inside, we'll see images of various deities; we may also see folks playing mahjong. A memorial service may be held in these temples, but it is unlikely that any of them are licensed to function as a funeral home in the American sense. As a compromise, an effigy of the deceased may be burned at the temple on behalf of the body in the funeral parlor.

When we see more formalized styles of Taoist ritual, he explains, the officiants are celibate monastic priests. In some understandings of Chinese traditional religion, there is concern that the dead be helped to heaven quickly, and not be left to languish in the hellish realm. A family may hire a Taoist priest to perform a very elaborate, multiple-stage (and sometimes, multiple-day) funeral ceremony through which various deities are given offerings, are told of the good deeds of the deceased, and are petitioned to forgive any debt incurred by wrongdoings. Paper effigies of the deceased and whatever he or she will need in the afterworld are burned; and a smooth transition is assured. America's Chinatowns include shops that specialize in selling things typically needed for a Taoist funeral, such as little houses, phones, radios, televisions, jewelry, and currency—all made of paper. Such ceremonies are *extremely* expensive. They do happen in American Chinese communities; but, Master Hon says, "this is only for very wealthy people. What my family did for my father is more typical."

When her grandfather died in New York a few years ago, what Dowoti Désir's family did was typical of Vodou practice— but with some twists. If her grandfather had died in Haiti, she points out, he would not have been buried in a cemetery but on his land, near the foundation of his house. Professor Désir officiated at her grandfather's funeral, adapting traditional rituals as necessary. Her son and his cousins had found a large, pink plastic heart that they wanted buried with him in his coffin. "I wanted them to do it in a way that would stay in their minds, that would give a sense of formality and closure. I recited a Yoruba prayer for the departed, and I invited everyone to mention the name of a lost ancestor. That piece of plastic is probably going to outlive his corpse! At the same time, it is symbolic of the kids' love for him, and that will outlive everything. So we have a sense that death doesn't terminate our relationships with those who have gone before us."

Vodou rites for the deceased vary from person to person, and certainly will differ when the person was an important leader or well-recognized elder, or a priest who had gone through initiation rites. Just as these mantles of authority were conferred through an initiatory process, Vodou provides a process of undoing of the bonds of authority ritually, so that the soul is no longer saddled with that responsibility. "It could be that actual ritual objects need to be transferred to someone else, who will become their caretaker," Professor Désir explains. "I have already informed my son that when something happens to me (because we're all going to die)—especially if it's an untimely thing—there are certain priests I want him to go see. I have shown him exactly what he has to give them. When someone dies, we have a process called *desoné*. It involves nail-trimming and the removal of hair from the head or armpits, because these are places of ongoing activity after death. It is a way of symbolically acknowledging this other place that you're in. Along with the trimming there are prayers to be said and cleansing to be done. When I die, there are things that will be necessary because the ritual of *desoné* is much more elaborate for a priest than for a layperson."

"*Soné* means literally 'to ring' a bell," she explains. "It's as if there is 'the bell' that creates the noise, that creates the vibration, that creates the dynamic, the energy that represents life. So, when you're alive, you are essentially *soné*. You see the movement of the bell swinging back and forth in our dance, in our ritual. It's almost as if you become the handle of God who is swinging you back and forth. The beauty, the power, the glory of that has resonance in the world. This is how we are animated. When we die, we are *desoné*. We're no longer ringing; we're no longer animated. We're no longer making that music, that joyful sound—as Christians like to refer to it. That is God's will, or the will of the *orisha*, because—again—we don't always go immediately to God. There's this little plane of ancestors and *orisha* or *lwa* in between. We're no longer their voice, in a manner of speaking."

"We need to pay homage to our ancestors," she insists. "We need to call their name. We need to *remember* them. We need to keep their spirit alive, even though we don't physically see. I believe my grandmother is behind me, and my great-grandmother is behind. I know they are within my reach. For example, this chair that I am sitting on—I don't allow other people to sit in it, and it usually stays empty, because it's *their* seat! It's their seat. Because we constantly need the guidance and the protection of our ancestors, we need to keep calling their names. When we stop calling their names, that's when they're really, really dead. Then *you* become dead, too, because you don't have them anymore; you don't have the benefit of their wisdom."

A Zen priest in Chicago recalls the traditional process his community undertook upon the passing of their senior teacher. "Our *roshi* died a wonderful, peaceful death in the *zendo* garden, surrounded by his students. His body was taken inside, stripped, and washed. While this was happening, there was chanting. No embalming fluid was used (out of respect for the body). He was put in his robes and laid to rest in the *zendo* for six days, kind of like being laid in state in an open coffin. The idea is that, if there *is* rebirth, you want to allow time for whatever is there to let go of the identity that is so tied up with the body. No one in the Zen community would claim that this is definitely what happens, but we have to allow for the possibility. On the death evening plus six more evenings, we held a memorial service. Each one of us had an opportunity to address our *roshi,* as though he were sitting there—because, in a way, he *was* sitting there; he was lying in state. There were a lot of tears and a lot of thanks. At the end of this period, he was buried. He simply was buried."

Cremation
The Zen community in Chicago buried their beloved teacher, but most Western Buddhists choose cremation. "Cremation has been the tradition from the Buddha's time until now," a Japanese Pure Land priest explains. "After the Buddha passed away, he was cremated. Then his ashes and bones were divided into eight parts and given to the kings of each of the regions in India." So the Buddha's bones are in various places now.

"A Buddhist funeral service is very simple," says the Venerable Kondanna, "but we all need some kind of ritual, no matter what background we are coming from. That is just to heal ourselves. When somebody is gone, we ask all the friends and family members to get together and perform some rituals from the ancient times." Cremation, however, is merely one step in a series of rituals.

The rituals from ancient times can sometimes be off-putting to modern sensibilities. A Buddhist chaplain recalls a day on which the young child of an Asian-American family had died in a Texas hospital. "A group of Tibetan monks arrived at the intensive care unit to attend to the child and his family. They wore their huge flowing robes and big yellow hats, and they came in chanting. The staff got really upset, and tried to block the monks from coming in. Our Christian chaplain interceded and the monks were able to enter. She told me, 'You know, I think that if it had been a group of Catholic monks, nobody would have cared.' That's just the fear we have of the other."

When a loved one is lost, says a member of New York's Chinese Pure Land community, "we don't cry; we are encouraged not to cry." The idea is to avoid agitating the deceased. "If the deceased person hears your cry, complete letting-go is not going to happen. We need to help the deceased person to let go, to be free."

"The ideal situation is to keep a nice, calm, peaceful atmosphere," a member of Wisconsin's Tibetan Buddhist community agrees—and members of other streams of Buddhism would concur as well. "It's best not to touch the body," he continues. "No loud sounds, no jolting or physical movement. If the person has been a strong practitioner, it is best if, after clinical death, the body can be left untouched, unmoved for three days." Is that possible in the American context? In most cases, says a Zen chaplain, no. "Most of the time in the West, especially in a hospital setting, with all the funding issues, you can't leave a body sitting in a room for several days."

But actually, sometimes the traditions *are* possible to maintain, as we saw with the Zen community in Chicago. It was the case as well when Geshe Thabkay, a much-loved teacher in Wisconsin's Tibetan Buddhist community, died a few years ago. "His body was able to stay mostly untouched and unmoved for three days," a lay practitioner points out. "Then his body was brought to a funeral home. All of us went there: monks, nuns, and laypeople. We did about an hour of prayer again, and then the cremation process started." Traditional Tibetan prayers continued for a while. "All of us were in the service room by the door to the furnace so that we could hear very clearly the sound of the cremation furnace as we did the prayers," he recalls. "It was a potent reminder again of one of the important points in Buddhism, that of our own and everyone's mortality." Then the ceremony became more typical of other American funerals. Everyone sat together in a pleasant room and took turns eulogizing their departed teacher.

Community members continued to meet daily to say prayers under the leadership of one of the monks for a full week after the teacher's death. "Geshe Thabkay himself had requested certain prayers to be said, so we did that," says a layman. "After that first week, monks in the monastery continued praying themselves."

"At a Buddhist funeral, you tend to have a lot of chanting," a chaplain notes. "Chanting could be understood as prayer (somewhat akin to Christianity), or it could be seen as meditation." While the Chicago Zen community favors the *Heart Sutra,* the Won Buddhist community in New York recites the Deliverance Prayer and does Deliverance chanting, a minister explains. "The body of the departing person has separated from the spirit. The moment of the spirit's departure is critical to rebirth. So the funeral focuses on preparing for the next life. We meditate with the body."

At a Theravada funeral, "monks may chant verses of impermanence, reminding that everything in this world is impermanent," notes the head of one American monastery. "Even though people know it, we always remind them. It is our opportunity to give them something to keep in their mind. Back and forth we go in our habit. We are habitual beings, so encouragement is given: Don't slip into old habits; be mindful. Mindfulness is key in Buddhist teaching."

When someone in the Japanese Pure Land community dies, explains the Reverend T. Kenjitsu Nakagaki, head priest of the New York Buddhist Church, "we go to the home, or the hospital, or wherever, and do last chanting. It might be right before death, but it might be right after. It's a bedside service. In the next day or so, traditionally, the body will be brought to the temple for *tsuya,* an all-night vigil. Family and friends gather and place incense, and a candle is kept burning overnight." Traditionally, the family would have taken care of the body, but now the funeral home does that. So, an American vigil is usually shortened and does not last all night.

Families often arrange for a viewing, Reverend Nakagaki notes, during which there will be some chanting of a *sutra* and some *nembutsu*—the Pure Land practice of calling upon Amitabha (the Buddha of Infinite Light) and Amitayus (the Buddha of Infinite Life—that is, Infinite Wisdom and Infinite Compassion). The *sutras* commonly chanted at the funeral differ from the *sutras* for the vigil, he explains. "For the funeral, we normally chant *sho-shin-ge,* which was actually written by Shinran, the founder of our school of Buddhism. We do it as regular chanting every day."

When faced with the death of a loved one, many American Buddhists turn to the *Bardo Thodol,* the Tibetan Book of the Dead—a very popular text among Western Buddhists of all stripes. One chaplain describes it as "a guided meditation which would help one's consciousness either to enlightenment or to a skillful, better rebirth." Guidance also may take the form of a *dharma* talk. "The way I see it," says a Theravada monk, "once somebody has gone away, he took whatever he did. Always we teach: when we die, we will not be carrying the material things with us; the only thing I will carry is the good *karma* of my good deeds. That is forming my next step, my next life. Therefore, when we talk at the funeral, we just remind everyone to be good. Nothing is important in all these material things. In Buddhist teachings, we are always encouraged to let go of things, holding on to nothing."

On the other hand, says a *sensei,* "at a Zen funeral, the message is directed at the deceased; and it is, primarily, the message of the *Heart Sutra:* 'This is One. Don't be deceived. You have nowhere to go. You are home. It is clear that you are afraid, because you are disembodied. But your sense of entity-ness, this longing, is not necessarily a positive thing.' It is the same message we deliver during life: 'Do not be entangled in your sense of self. Do not take that so seriously, so literally.' So there is guidance, but the guidance is less directed toward a good rebirth *per se* than in some other Buddhist traditions."

In Theravada tradition, monks renounce all of their possessions when they leave home to be ordained. "But they still need a piece of cloth to wear," a monk points out, and when that piece becomes tattered, it needs to be replaced. "In ancient times, most mendicants picked up stuff at the funeral grounds." Now "funeral clothes" are actually gifts to the monks in memory of that person who has gone," he explains. "Nowadays, normally, the family of the deceased will buy a robe and offer it to monks. Very simple."

When a Shinto-follower dies, it is quite common for the family to arrange for a Buddhist funeral. However, the Reverend Koichi Barrish points out, Shinto does have a *shinsosai,* a funeral ceremony. "Here at the Tsubaki Shrine of America, we have conducted a number of such rituals," he says. Actually, a Shinto funeral is a series of ceremonies, beginning with a vigil. "In Shinto, having a vigil recognizes that the *mitama,* the soul, is getting used to the idea of not being alive anymore," Reverend Barrish says. "It can kind of look around, and be in the presence of family and friends, and ease that transition, then go off on the path, becoming more spiritualized." The vigil also acknowledges that although this person is dead and is not coming back, family and friends can sense that the *mitama* is still there. Next comes the *senrei-sai,* the ceremony of transferring the *mitama* from the body to a *mitama-shiro,* a specially prepared memorial plaque. "Then there is the *shinsosai*—the funeral ceremony itself," Reverend Barrish explains. "That is done in front of this memorial plaque." There is also a ceremony for seeing the body off at the time of cremation, and another ceremony for the people returning home.

Traditionally, these funeral ceremonies would take place in the home of the deceased person rather than in the shrine proper. However, Reverend Barrish clarifies, there are rituals for the dead that can be, and often are, done on the shrine grounds. "We set up a temporary shrine in our reception area, but we don't go into the shrine building itself. We can't do anything on the shrine grounds involving the body. In fact, if a Shinto priest does the actual ceremony of the transfer of the *mitama* from the body to the *mitama-shiro,* in such a case, the priest cannot return to the shrine in that day. Likewise, the ritual clothing he wore cannot return to the shrine grounds. We have the big guesthouse structure on the shrine property, but it is across the street from the shrine itself. So, I have a place I can go after doing such a ceremony, and it includes a place where I can store that clothing."

American Shinto-followers try to avoid embalming by opting for cremation. Cremation is the common practice in Japan as well, so this is not an innovation. Customarily, the ashes are buried rather than sprinkled or spread, but, Reverend Barrish stresses, "the ashes never come near to the shrine." The ashes of a corpse would defile the shrine? "Exactly," he nods.

"The most important thing is to understand the nature of life and death from a Shinto perspective," he stresses, "and to try to ameliorate the terrible disconnect that results from typical American practices around death. People are whisked away. The fact that there is no time for the family to be with the body after passing is bad for the family, and it's bad for the *mitama*. Depending on the spirituality and clarity of the particular *mitama* of that person, it could be pretty horrific for the *mitama* to try to make its way between worlds, and to get used to the idea of not being in the body anymore without some time with the family. The fascinating thing about Shinto practices around death is that they are *for* the *mitama*. They are not just for the people who remain here to feel better. They are actually *for* the *mitama*."

"Before the disposal of the body," says a Michigan Hindu, "we follow almost the same procedure adopted by many other faiths. This means bathing and wrapping the body—preferably in a white cloth without seams. It should not be sewn." In Hindu tradition, the body is to be kept as intact as possible until it is cremated. "In India," he continues, "we would lay the body in a respectful manner on a custom-made wooden plank. Here, we use a casket. Then we take the body to the cremation place. A priest should recite some verses from the Vedas, our oldest scripture. After the recitation, we perform certain oblations on the body. Wood, melted butter, certain herbs—members of the family put these on the body. Then the body is completely burned up. In the Western world, the body is placed in a crematorium—an electric furnace. It is okay for family members to leave, but there should be one person who stays until the body is completely burned up. After three days, you can collect the ashes, and the ashes are to be put in a river. The water should be flowing; it should not be standing."

Hindus have been settling in the New Orleans area since the 1960s. "Our local cemetery has become accustomed to the Hindu community and now knows how to accommodate our preferences," explains the manager of one of the city's temples. "It has a crematorium. They let us do our rituals there. We bathe the body. We purify the body." In this community, the actual funeral *puja* is conducted by a professor of physics who is also a Hindu priest.

"Most of us Hindus believe in cremation," the temple manager continues. "We believe that when we die, our body returns to the five basic elements: earth, water, air, fire, and space. The basic idea we have in cremating the body is that the body will vanish, and you will no longer occupy the space. That is the fifth element. We don't want to occupy space when we are not supposed to." Indeed, the leader of a Michigan congregation concurs. "You can burn thousands and thousands of corpses in the space where one body could be buried."

"Ultimately we're all supposed to be made out of the fire element," a Hindu chaplain explains, "so when people die, that's the reason they're cremated. It's much quicker to go back to our elemental state if everything is burnt down. If it is buried, it will take longer. But to make doubly sure, we take the ashes and blow some of them in the air and the water, and some are spread over the earth. And then we offer both a thanksgiving and an apology to the deceased—thanksgiving in the sense that when we breathe, we will be taking part of their element into ourselves. And that is a thanksgiving because they give us some sustenance, too. Their element has come back to us. So in a way, we get incarnated every time somebody dies, because of that element we breathe in."

When his aunt died recently, a professor explains, she was taken to a nearby funeral home in her Midwestern suburb. "There was an attempt to do pre-cremation rituals Hindus perform in India, such as walking around the corpse, and putting rice in the mouth of the corpse, and saying mantras. A priest was there, of course, to assist in all this. It was interesting how people dressed. I wore the traditional *pyjama kurta,* the loose pants and the loose white top, thinking that it was what was appropriate for a Hindu ceremony. But many of our friends and relatives were dressed in Western-style clothing. It was a blending of worlds."

In India, the oldest son would light the funeral pyre. In an American cremation, there is no pyre to light. "When the casket is closed, we usually put a little oil lamp with a cotton wick on top of the casket," a Louisiana engineer explains. "This symbolizes the cremation fire. Then we push the casket in, and the machine takes over." Some Hindus have the oldest son push the crematorium button instead. "My aunt's eldest son pressed the switch," the Midwestern professor recalls, "and then somebody touched him, and somebody touched that person, and so on— so that everyone got the sense that they were pressing the switch together."

Similar to America's Hindus, America's Jains use electric cremation, a family member having cleansed the body first. The traditional Indian practice is to cremate the body very quickly after death—primarily because the climate promotes rapid decomposition. While Hindus believe in depositing the ashes of their deceased loved ones in a river, Jains do not. That would pollute the water, a Jain obstetrician explains. Would American Jains hold a funeral service? "That is social and cultural," says an internist. But, says a pediatrician, "we'll have something at the temple. At our temple here, when a community member dies, there is a *puja,* a special ceremony, for a couple of hours. The community comes in and pays respect to the soul of the departed and prays for that soul."

When death occurs in a Zoroastrian family, the hope is that someone will take note of the exact time. This information will be important later on, since there will be anniversaries to mark. A Zoroastrian day runs from sunrise to sunrise, so memorials of a death that occurred at 3:00 a.m. on December 1 of the secular calendar, for example, will actually take place on November 30. In a traditional Zoroastrian home, no food is cooked during the interval between the death of family member and the disposal of the body, and the bereaved abstain from meat. Friends and relatives make sure meals are brought in.

America's larger Zoroastrian communities will have a *darbe mehr*, a place where they gather for communal worship, fellowship, and education. However, Zoroastrian funerals are never conducted there, a Chicago priest explains. "We cannot have any funeral at the *darbe mehr* because of our conviction that when the person dies, the body disintegrates. It is not ritually pure, and it should not come in touch with anything that is ritually pure."

Actually, Zoroastrians hold not one, but many services when someone dies. For most of them, a priest notes, the body is not present. For the first four days, there are specific prayers to help the soul of the deceased with the different stages through which it is passing, and those rituals may be held at the *darbe mehr*. "We have some services on the night of the disposal of the body. We have a ceremony on the third evening, and another on the fourth dawn, when we believe the soul is passing over the Chinvat Bridge, the Bridge of Separation."

"When I was the only priest in the Chicago area, I conducted all of the funerals," Dr. Kersey Antia explains. "But now we have many priests, so it depends on our convenience and people's choice. We have trained all of our priests to conduct funerals." During these ceremonies, the priest should avoid facing north (the direction of fierce winter wind and invaders in the religion's native Persia); the body should not point northward either. Since a funeral cannot happen at a *darbe mehr*, "we have made arrangements with a funeral home to allow us to use the facility," he says.

Zoroastrians do not embalm the body. "Our belief is that your soul is going to move on," a medical student explains. When someone dies, prayers are recited, the body is washed, and then the *sudreh* and *kusthi*—the traditional undergarment and waistcord—are put back on the person. "We would not embalm because that would be introducing something artificial into the person after you've already cleansed them," she says. "The body is not on show for anybody. There is no viewing, which might be the thought behind embalming."

"Until recently, in the old world, prayers were held near the body until the funeral, and thereafter until the fourth dawn near the place where the body was placed," Dr. Antia explains. In America, there are some modifications. "We keep a candle near the body through the night," he says. "The body must have light." The funeral prayer takes at least an hour, he explains, and consists of the first *Gatha,* the longest of the prayers of Zarathustra. Traditionally, Zoroastrian prayer is performed in front of an urn of fire, but since the funeral home will not allow this, he notes, they substitute a candle.

When it comes to Zoroastrian funerals, a medical student says, "one thing that is pretty consistent is the prayers. The order of the prayers might vary a little, but the prayers are the prayers. Here in America, there is some variation between the Iranian and Parsi Zoroastrians. The majority of Zoroastrians are in India, Iran, and Pakistan. Our practices are quite different from theirs. We have had to adapt, which many of them find hard to accept. Some of them tell us we are not 'really Zoroastrian' because of the adaptations we have had to make. The prayers are the same, but the manner in which we dispose of the dead is not the same."

The traditional custom of placing the body on a Tower of Silence is maintained in some parts of India, but most Zoroastrians in the North American community choose cremation. This is a matter of some community debate. "It used to be frowned upon," a medical student explains. "Fire is holy for us, so placing a corpse on a fire would be wrong. It would be putting contamination into something we consider sacred. But here, we have electrical crematoriums that don't use flame."

"Sikhs are taught that once the soul leaves the body, the body is not that important anymore," explains a Michigan educator. "The body is just the repository for the soul. You still treat the body with dignity, but ultimately it is something you dispose of once the soul leaves. Guru Nanak is our founding prophet. When he died, he was beloved by both the Hindu and the Muslim communities. Each wanted to treat his body in its own way. The Hindus wanted to cremate him and the Muslims wanted to bury him. They argued, but when they lifted the shroud, there was no body left underneath. The point of that parable is not the miracle of the body disappearing, but that what we do with the body isn't critical. What we do while the body is alive and the soul is inhabiting it—*that* is what's important. That said, there are traditions which have evolved as to what we do at the time of death."

"In India, most deaths take place at home, rather than the hospital," explains a professor, "so even when death occurs in the hospital, the body would be brought home. It is then bathed in milk and water by family members of the same gender." A place for the body is prepared, often in the living room. "It is placed on the floor—not on a bed. If the body is to stay overnight, you keep reciting prayers. Family members will sleep on the floor next to the body. It is not left alone."

These customs have been modified in the American context, says a leader of the Michigan community. "Traditionally, Sikhs are cremated," she notes. "What we are told to do at the time of death is to focus on prayer—singing of prayer, reading of prayer. What will normally happen is that we will say a prayer at the funeral home, prior to cremation. At the very minimum it will be the *Sohila* prayer, which is in fact our night prayer, but it is also a reminder of death—that the soul will leave its home and go eternally forward. Then we will go to the *gurdwara*. We'll say the *Ardas*. That is the main prayer we say at the end of every function. Maybe they'll have a couple of hymns sung. The hymns surrounding death are always about how we need to be preparing ourselves; as we are here on earth, we need to be doing the good deeds, the meditation, so that when our time comes, our soul is prepared to leave and to go on its journey."

"In India," says a nurse, "the cremation happens in an open area. The body is placed on the wood and is covered with a single white sheet. The body is burned the same day that the person died, so there is no embalming or storage of the body. The son is supposed to light the pyre. Women don't go to the cremation grounds. They stay at home or in the *gurdwara*. After the body is burned, everyone comes back to the *gurdwara* to do the final prayer."

In America it is different, she points out. "The funeral will be postponed for a day or two, so that people can come to pay their respects and view the body. Many American Sikhs hold a 'viewing'—which does not happen in India. Sometimes they will even wait for people to come from India, or wherever else in the States, so that they can all be there for the cremation. More and more, I think, people realize that family members need to be present to say goodbye." In such a case, some Sikhs embalm, she notes, "but there are some families here who will not. I have known a couple of families here whose parents have said, 'We don't want our bodily fluids taken out of our body' (because bodily fluids are taken out to embalm). They don't care if something is put in, but they don't want anything taken out."

Death's Demands

An important dimension of what we have described here few outsiders will ever see: the ritual washing and anointing of the corpse prescribed by almost every religion. The details of these washings differ, sometimes dramatically. In the preface, we heard of FEMA's effort to conduct ceremonial washings of hurricane victims. This was noble, but it is unlikely that a single method could honestly comply with the requirements of multiple religions. Nevertheless, FEMA was attempting what all of these ceremonies intend: to honor the deceased; to preserve dignity in the face of loss.

Gradually, as the neighborhoods they serve become more religiously complex, funeral homes in many American cities have become more accommodating of a wider range of needs and expectations around the various approaches to washing, the reasons for eschewing embalming, and the ways in which family members want to participate. Whereas just a few years ago the family would have to bring any required ritual items, some funeral homes now have these things on hand. Mourners may prefer to sit on the floor, so some funeral homes now have a hall from which pews or chairs can be removed easily. An American cremation will take place in an indoor chamber; there will be no open-air fire to kindle. Many funeral directors now understand that their Hindu, Buddhist, Jain, and Sikh clients may want a designated family member to push the "start" button. Accepting guidance on these matters from local congregations and religious leaders has actually helped business, some funeral directors report. This is not entirely novel: American funeral homes have long adapted to customs of new immigrant groups. However, it is only in the past few decades that this has meant something other than accommodating new expressions of Christianity.

Death always places demands on the surviving family, but the demands are more complex when it is not just the neighborhood, but the family itself, that is multireligious. "This brings me to a point about America's indigenous Muslims—how important it is that we have some document stating how we Muslim converts want to be buried," an imam stresses. "Many of us have a dual family system. You might have a Christian parent or wife, or Jewish family members. You have been practicing Islam for thirty or forty years, but then here you are at the end of life, and in comes Aunt Susan with a Bible in her hand, reminding you that you were first born a Christian, and saying she's going to bury you as a Christian! That's traumatic for a dying person to hear. I have been an advocate for having something similar to a healthcare proxy, so this person can say, 'This is what I want to be buried as.'" It makes the dying person feel more comfortable, and—whatever the family does—it assures the community of faith that they have done their best to honor this person's last wishes.

The family will have responsibilities for the affairs of the deceased long after the funeral rituals have been completed—and some of these responsibilities may well be spiritual. It is to aspects of remembrance that we now turn.

CHAPTER FIVE

Recovery

WE HAVE EXPLORED some of the rituals that mark the end of life for adherents of various religions, but what provisions are made for those who are left behind? For them the journey of suffering continues with its own heartaches and challenges, "and it is stunning to realize how long the pain lingers," notes one grieving father. And what about times when loss is massive and multireligious? Here too, as Elisabeth Kübler-Ross has taught us, human beings move gradually and in spiral fashion from shock and denial through anger and depression to acceptance. During the grieving process, one Jewish psychologist explains, "you have to do two things at once: you have to feel the pain, and you have to heal from the pain. The key is to interrelate the two effectively." In this chapter we will consider how religions provide philosophical and ceremonial ways of helping the bereaved cope with the pain that lingers, and of encouraging the healing process to begin.

Mourning at the Time of Death

While the funeral brings closure of one sort, the sting of loss is still fresh. Many religions acknowledge that by providing practices for the first few days or weeks after a death. Sometimes these practices are linked to that religion's teachings on what happens to the individual upon death; at other times, they are ways of recognizing that the bereaved need some time and space to adjust.

Common to most streams of Buddhism is the custom of holding a memorial service on the seventh day after a person's death. "On the sixth night after someone dies," a Theravada monk explains, "we do a *dhamma* sermon, an instructional talk; then on the seventh day, we do *dana*—which means 'giving,' or 'merit-making.'" The family of the deceased may come to the *vihara* to make offerings to the Buddha, after which they and the monks sit together and chant. *Dana* might include preparing lunch for the monks in memory of the departed loved one, and then offering food to any other people who are present. It could just as well involve taking food to someone in a nursing home or hospital. "They share. That's how they do it," the monk says. Or, the monks can go to the people. "Tuesday, our abbot went to New Jersey. One of our devout ladies died suddenly of a heart attack. The seven-day *dana* took place that day." That is, the family of the deceased had invited the abbot for lunch.

When the Cherokee community loses a member, a healer explains, "the death song is sung four times: on the day you find out the person is dead, at the funeral, four days after, and seven days after. Usually, on the seventh day, the family of the deceased is 'taken to water.' 'Going to Water' is a ceremony of purification and cleansing yourself. The water is associated with the north, with the color blue—the color of sadness and depression. Blue is also the color of water, which washes those things away. So we take the family to water. The grieving process actually lasts a year. For that year, you don't say the person's name. You use some kind of euphemism instead. Then that process of 'Going to Water' is done again."

Among the Mohawk people it is the custom for members of some other clan to relieve the clanspeople of the deceased of their daily chores for the first nine days. "They work for us and cook for us and clean for us for nine days," says a chief. "Then, on the tenth day, that family who lost somebody, *they* do the cooking and *they* feed all the people for all the work they did; and they give them gifts. Usually, the gifts are from whatever belonged to the person who died: shoes, socks, a radio—whatever they had. They call it a Give-Away."

In a traditional Zoroastrian home, an oil lamp or candle is kept burning near the bed of the deceased for at least ten days. Flowers might also be placed nearby, although some families feel it is more "Zoroastrian" to make a donation to charity in lieu of flowers. "As Zoroastrians, we're not really supposed to grieve," a medical student explains. "The idea is that the longer you grieve, the longer that soul is not happy. This delays it from making its way up to God. You're holding it back. We have the four days of prayers when a person dies. The fourth day is sort of a farewell. Then there is a special prayer on the tenth day."

"We believe that when we die, our soul hovers around the house or the family for twelve days," explains a Hindu engineer. "In India, we would have a continuous prayer service for twelve days, from morning to evening. Here in America, we just do it in the evening. We do *bhajans* and *kirtans*—songs of praise and devotion—and a prayer service. We have a priest do special rituals. We believe that, after twelve days, the soul goes away." One tradition is to make offerings of things like flowers, sweets, and rice balls. The hope is that a crow will come and take the food away. After twelve days, there are rituals for the eldest son to perform. "When my father passed away," he recalls, "I did the ritual for about five hours. It involves bathing two or three times, and doing *puja*. I am a nuclear engineer by profession. I never believed in such things. But when you go through such experiences, then you feel that maybe some form of energy is there."

Traditionally, once a Sikh family member has been cremated, a professor explains, "everyone comes to your home. You have had the house cleaned. Then you bring the *Guru Granth Sahib*—the Sikh holy book—to your house, which makes everything beautiful. And now, there will be a complete reading of the scripture, from first page to last, most likely for forty-eight hours nonstop. Different people will recite: professional reciters, friends, relatives, women and men alike. One person stops, and another will pick up on that line. What is nice about this is that you don't have to make small talk. The recitation is going on continuously. People just stop by, hear it, and go off. The presence of the *Guru Granth Sahib* provides solace. It is very nice, because what can you say? There is nothing to say. So, silence, sitting, hearing the sacred word: that is the ritual."

This practice ties in with the tradition of condolence calls, which are such a part of Indian culture, regardless of religion, and which many Indians maintain in America. "It is really important to pay that condolence call when someone passes," a Sikh educator explains. It facilitates the grieving process, because you are able to vent, to cry, multiple times. It's an opportunity for them to sit down and read a little bit. Friends will bring food by. It varies."

In her community, says a nurse, the reading of the whole *Guru Granth Sahib* often stretches over nine or eleven days. In some families, prayers are part of this ritual. Once the reading is completed, family and friends assemble for a memorial service and *langar*—the traditional sharing of food. "Now the shock phase is over," she explains, "so the discussion turns to what practical things the family needs now, to get used to their life without this person. That's the kind of thing that's decided."

The grieving process is helped by *kirtan*—the singing of the sacred hymns from scripture, explains a businesswoman. "The *kirtan* at the funeral home is usually short," she says, "and it's intense, because the body is still there. This is the goodbye. The *kirtan* is still intense when you go to the memorial service five or seven or thirteen days later, because the loss is still fresh. A lot of *shabads,* or hymns, in the *Guru Granth Sahib* pertain to death. They aren't *about* death. They're about how we should be living our life. They're a reminder to us that we are all going to die."

It may strike the onlooker that traditional Jews know exactly what they are supposed to do when death strikes the family. Indeed, says an Orthodox educator, the Jewish grieving process begins once the body is buried. It has several stages, the first of which is called *shivah*—a seven-day period of intense mourning. "With *shivah*, there is a formula. You know the formula; you do the formula; and the formula is comforting. Having people around is comforting (for the most part). Sometimes it can be overwhelming. It can feel like you have to entertain people. But you shouldn't have to. You focus on your loss. The community is there for you—which is a real blessing."

"Death seems to provoke a need to do things right," says a Reconstructionist rabbi. "I have found that even if they haven't been living an observant lifestyle, when a family loses a loved one, they want to know the traditions. They want to know what to do." A Reform cantor agrees. "The very prescriptive elements can be incredibly helpful. Sometimes people are feeling lost. Often people who never show up to synagogue on a Friday night, all of a sudden feel very connected Jewishly when they lose someone who is close to them. So, being told that 'this is what Jews do when they are in mourning' can be very helpful. A lot of my people don't know what the formula is, but they are relieved to know that there is a formula, and that they can follow it."

Customarily, upon returning home from the cemetery, the grieving family lights a special seven-day memorial candle and eats a simple "meal of consolation" provided by friends. This symbolizes the need for the healing process to begin. Traditionally, the family will stay in the house throughout *shivah*. The mourners sit on low benches, which funeral homes can provide. Explanations for this custom vary: it may indicate submission to God's will, or nearness to the earth in which the deceased has just been buried, or simply that things are not "normal" right now. Everyone else will sit on regular furniture. In a traditional *shivah* house, the mirrors will be covered. "Traditional Jews will be wearing clothing they have torn at the graveside—ripped clothes! They will sit in those clothes the entire week. They will not shower; they will not wear real shoes; men will not shave; no haircuts; no studying Torah. Traditional mourners really do look like they are in an altered state, especially as the week wears on."

What about the visitor to a *shivah* house? "You come in and sit down; you wait until the mourner addresses you first," she advises. "The idea is to talk about the person who has died, to share stories and talk about the loss. People are there to listen to you."

"One of the first things you learn about pastoral care in trauma and disaster is to get people to tell their stories," Rabbi Blanchard points out. "This has been built into the Jewish way of doing things for ages. It works. In the beginning, the stories are not well formed, you're reaching for things. But you begin to heal. By the time *shivah* is over, you really have begun the narrative that includes your loved one's death."

It is a community responsibility to make certain there is a *minyan* for daily ritual prayers, which include the recital of the Mourner's *Kaddish.* For the Orthodox, this means ten male adults; other Jews count women in the *minyan.* "I lead *shivah minyans* at the homes of congregants," says a Reform cantor. "I leave the books in the home, and I come and lead the evening *minyan.* So if they want to do the morning one, they are on their own. Many people in our congregation come from a secular background, so this isn't something they are familiar with. I have seen it be transformative for visitors who happen to be there then, and also for the family—because they receive support from places where they don't necessarily expect to receive it. They are allowing that support to come in by saying, 'We are sitting *shivah,* and we will be conducting a *shivah minyan.*' They are allowing people the opportunity to do the *mitzvah* of showing up and offering their support." Comforting mourners is considered a meritorious act.

Even though *shivah* means seven, the period is really only six days long, because there is always a Sabbath in there and according to Jewish law, *Shabbat* and mourning are mutually contradictory. When the Sabbath is about to begin, explains Talmud scholar Devorah Zlochower, "you take a break. You shower; you put on your *Shabbat* clothes; you go to synagogue."

The Friday night service is somewhat more joyous than the Saturday service, so the custom in many synagogues is for mourners to stay outside until the transition from Sabbath Welcoming to Evening Service itself. "When the mourners walk into the synagogue," she explains, "the community stands up, turns to them, and greets them." The greeting here is the same one used by any visitor when departing from a *shivah* house: "May God comfort you among the mourners of Zion and Jerusalem" (among Ashkenazi Jews) or "May you be comforted from heaven" (among the Sephardi). "There is definitely a huge sense of solidarity at those moments," she stresses.

"There's a certain genius to this kind of a ceremony," says Rabbi Blanchard, "because it pairs the pain with its cure. In fact, that is one of the principles of behavior therapy. Sometimes you have to excite the thing you want to extinguish; so you pair it with its opposite, and it goes away! And it's interesting. In traditional Jewish circles, even on *Shabbat* you are allowed to cry. Why? Because it relieves the pain. You cry because it makes you feel better, not worse."

The last day of *shivah* ends by about noontime. Traditionally, Ms. Zlochower explains, "people will perform the Morning Prayer services, then they'll 'get up from *shivah*' by taking a walk around the block, which is symbolic of reintegration into the larger community. Then they shower, change, and go to work or whatever. People often say that the week after *shivah* is really hard because at that point you're on your own. That is when the loss really hits."

Whereas *Shabbat* interrupts *shivah* for a twenty-five-hour period, the major Jewish holidays of *Rosh ha-Shanah, Yom Kippur, Sukkot, Simchat Torah, Pesach,* and *Shavuot* (but not *Chanukah* or *Purim*) actually end it. Having *shivah* cancelled by a holiday is not seen as a blessing, one rabbi admits. He recalls a friend whose mother died at one o'clock of the day on which Passover was to begin at sundown. She was buried that afternoon. "Her son had only an hour of *shivah,* then he got up. He said, 'I'm not allowed to act like a mourner, but a mourner's heart is a mourner's heart.'"

Members of the Conservative, Reconstructionist, and Reform movements may follow all of these customs, but some do not. Sitting *shivah* is supposed to be consoling, not burdensome, so some Jews (for various reasons) may choose to sit only the first three days of mourning (as these are considered the most intense); most rabbis would recommend this as a minimum, but some Jews elect to sit *shivah* only one day. Mirrors might be left uncovered. Mourners might sit on regular chairs. A torn black ribbon might represent torn clothing. Women will be counted in the *minyan* for saying the Mourner's *Kaddish.* "You can pick and choose," a professor notes.

"Some things would be the same," says a Reform cantor. "In many Reform houses, you would have water outside, for people to wash their hands. People coming to a *shivah*-house would not be expected to knock on the door or ring the bell. That would be the same. There is always a huge spread of food. One of the things I encourage my congregants to do is to allow the mourner to *sit.* Feel free to go into their kitchen and do the dishes. Don't ask; just go do it. This is something that is new to a lot of people in my congregation, because I think a lot of us are not used to letting people take care of us. On the other side of it, when a friend loses someone, you often feel you want to help, but you don't know how. That is what is so wonderful about *shivah.* It offers an opportunity for people to do things that will be helpful—and you don't even have to ask; you can just do them!"

Mourning a Child

The loss of a child brings with it a special degree of grief, a Sikh nurse affirms, but "most Sikhs would remember that we don't know how much suffering the child would have had, had he survived. You have to let him go back to God, because the child was never yours in the first place. You are just getting the duty to help him through, while he's on this earth." That is an important point to reach, she stresses, "because one does have to survive the death of a child."

"Muslims don't believe in original sin," a Michigan imam emphasizes. "We believe that a child is born pure." Anyone who dies as an infant or a child is believed to have died sinless. "So we pray for the parents; we ask God to bless the parents," he says. "God decides things, and everything has a purpose.

Sometimes we know about it; sometimes we don't. But we do believe that he knows best." A chaplain agrees. "God says that if a child should pass before the mother," a Muslim chaplain notes, "the mother will already have a place in Paradise. See how helpful it is for the woman to know that? That God says in the Qur'an that you already have the gates of Paradise open for you?"

"When someone in our community has lost a child, we practice the Japanese Water Baby Ceremony," explains Sensei Sevan Ross, a Zen priest in Chicago. "A 'water baby' is a fetus, but it can mean a child, too. The ceremony is quite long, complicated, and very private." Parents of a deceased child can participate whenever they are ready. To begin, they are given a sweet, child-like *Jizo* statue. "As part of the ceremony, the parents make little capes and little hats and things out of red cloth for *Jizo*, who is clearly a substitute for their child. Then they dress this figure and then pull it through water."

"The Water Baby Ceremony is simply the most healing thing I have ever seen," Sensei Ross declares. "Parents spend an hour or two sewing this clothing with eight, ten, twelve people—all of whom have lost a child. In fact, in our case, we don't let anybody in the room unless they've lost a child. During the ceremony, there are no questions and answers. Someone might just say, 'The name of my child was Billy.' There will be more tears. Once the clothing is made, they chant a special chant for the loss of a child. It's in Japanese, and it is probably untranslatable. I have seen this ceremony reduce strapping men to puddles of tears, and they'll come back weeks later and say, 'That was one of the best things I ever did in my life. I finally had a chance to grieve publicly with other people who were having a chance to grieve publicly.' It is one of Japanese Buddhism's best contributions to the grieving process."

"At our temple," he continues, "we allow parents to take the *Jizo* figure home for forty-nine days. In some communities, the figure is buried; in others, it is burned. In Japan, it is traditional to leave it outside for up to a year. A Zen community in Oregon does it that way. When you do that, the clothing withers and rots, and finally just disappears. This is how we honor and release these children that have been lost, whether through abortion or miscarriage or through early death."

Judaism's laws around public mourning for infants, a Conservative rabbi notes, stem from a time when infant mortality and death in childbirth were much more prevalent. "If a child does not live for thirty days, tradition says we are not to do the full public ritual. The reality is that the parents are still facing an unspeakable loss, but the community is not there for them. In some Jewish circles, new rituals have been invented to repair this. There are now Jewish rituals for miscarriages, for example. These have emerged as women have assumed roles of religious leadership. We are developing new patterns of ritual to accommodate new patterns of loss."

The Mid-Stages of Grieving

Just as they often ritualize the first steps of addressing loss, religions may also ritualize the need to move toward reestablishment of one's normal routine. Thus there may be customs to observe for the first month or two following the funeral. For example, in a traditional Zoroastrian home, the possessions of the deceased would be left in place for at least a month, in case the soul still has some attachment to these things. In America, however, traditions such as this are falling away. Jews may observe *sloshim*—a thirty-day period of less intense mourning. These thirty days include *shivah,* an Orthodox rabbi clarifies, "so you've got twenty-three days left. There are still some restrictions on you. However, they're less rigorous, so you're back into the game a little bit." And, as with *shivah,* a major holiday cancels *sloshim.*

Thirty days after the death of a loved one, Jains may hold a *Panch Kalyanak Puja.* This approximately two-hour ceremony commemorates the Five Great Events in the life of the *tirthankara* Mahavira: his conception, his birth, his becoming a renunciate, his attaining omniscience, and his achieving *mok-*

sha—liberation. *Panch Kalyanak Pujas* can be held on any important occasion. So, Indubhai Dhruv explains, the remembrance he is holding this morning for his mother at the Jain Center of America is essentially identical to the ceremony that took place in India on the day after her death a month ago. The difference, he says, is that, in India, professionals did everything; essentially, the family were spectators. Here, family members and friends, even the children, make the ritual offerings of eight substances, each rich with symbolism: water, sandalwood, flowers, incense, light, rice, sweets, and fruit. The *pujari* guides them and plays a metal percussion instrument to signal the end of a stage in the ritual and the beginning of the next. The congregation joins the chanting, and hymn-singing accompanies and follows each offering. Each song has a message, Mr. Dhruv explains during the luncheon afterward. "One of the songs was telling us, 'Life is short; don't take it for granted. If something is important, do it now!'"

Like Jains, Theravada Buddhists hold a ceremony of remembrance on the thirtieth day, but Mahayana Buddhists do so every seven days until the forty-ninth day, with a special ceremony at the end of the series. "Forty-nine days seems to be a reasonably human time to open the grieving process up so it can 'drain,'" says the priest of a Chicago *zendo*. Zen Buddhism is less formal about these things than some other streams, but the bereaved in Zen communities sometimes do observe a forty-nine-day practice. At a *zendo* in Michigan, it is common for the community to gather for a memorial service after the forty-ninth day. "We bring a favorite food of the deceased person to share as we talk about him or her."

For Won Buddhists, these forty-nine days provide "a period of building peace, healing wounds, fixing unresolved issues," a minister explains. "We visit the family during this time. Once a week, the family comes to the temple for a Deliverance Service. At the end of the forty-nine days, there is the Deliverance and Saying Goodbye Service. Family members prepare a statement to the deceased person. It is a very moving experience, a chance to say *whatever* you never got to say. There is a lot of ritual. This is a time of energy-communication, so it is critical to have a good master facilitating. All of this is just as important as the funeral," she stresses.

As Tibetan Buddhists understand it, a person's "subtle consciousness" may abide in the *bardo* up to forty-nine days following *actual* death—that is, the point when that subtle consciousness separated itself from the physical body. "The *bardo* may be likened to a dream state in which one has a nonphysical body," a member of Wisconsin's Deer Park community explains. "Every seven days, if the right *karmic* causes and conditions come about, the consciousness has the opportunity to take rebirth into the next lifetime. The type of rebirth depends on the *karmic* impulses dominating at that time. At the forty-ninth day, the rebirth will definitely take place, if it hasn't already." Indeed, sometimes rebirth happens immediately after death, a Pure Land priest agrees, "but by the time of the forty-ninth day, the deceased are well settled into their next life."

As do many forms of Buddhism, Taoism provides a forty-nine-day practice for the bereaved. Taoists keep the deceased loved one's photograph on display for a forty-nine-day mourning period, says a *Qigong* master. "Every day, in the morning, you bring incense and a glass of water." His widowed mother continues to do this with a photo of his deceased father. "Believe me," he says, "he is now the best husband there is, because he is there to listen to her attentively. And he doesn't talk back. My father, after his passing, has become a perfect husband!" The point he wants to make, however, is this. "Taoism teaches that you may have lost a loved one, but you should continue to feel his or her being in your own self. At the end of the period, you put seven grains of rice in the water, and then you pour it out on a special plant you have bought. In this way, you work with grieving." A priest may be summoned to perform the Seventh Day Ritual, and again every seven days until the "seventh Seven," the ritual for which is longer than the others.

While Buddhists and Taoists mark the first forty-nine days of loss, Shinto-followers mark the first fifty. After a Shinto funeral, the family brings home the *mitama-shiro*, the memorial plaque to which the soul of the deceased has been ritually transferred. "Each day for fifty days, they can say a special prayer in front of it, and a special prayer each evening," a priest explains.

"Those prayers are the *O harai no Kotoba,* the Great Words of Purification, as well as the *Mitama Shizume no Kotoba,* the Words of Soul Pacification." In addition, there are ceremonies to be conducted by a priest on the tenth, twentieth, thirtieth, fortieth, and fiftieth days.

While this fifty-day process of regular ceremonies is primarily for the benefit of the *mitama,* obviously it is also of tremendous benefit to the family. "It's a great thing—something the family can actually do," he affirms. "The sense is that the *mitama* is rising spiritually, but it is also really around. The deceased person is not quite in this realm, but not quite gone either." That is why it is traditional for someone to be at home with the *mitama* around the clock until that fifty-day process is over. This vigil, Shinto-followers believe, prevents the deceased person from becoming confused. "The family can really feel the presence of the *mitama.* They really can communicate. They know they are aiding the transition process."

One chief explains that, while members of the Mohawk community are supposed to stop mourning on the tenth day after the death of a loved one, "they are allowed to 'semi-mourn' for a year." As the bereaved move from shock of loss to the mid-stages of grieving, our neighbors' religions talk about and facilitate this need to "semi-mourn" in various ways.

"You know, in a time of struggle, in a time of bereavement, Muslims find comfort in the teaching that all comes from Allah, and for everything we say *al-Hamdu li-Llah*—All Praise Be to God," a community activist reminds us. "But then, we're human, so we also have stories about the tears the Prophet shed at the loss of his son Ibrahim. The human anguish of grieving is acknowledged. It happened even to the Prophet—which is of comfort for some Muslims. 'I know that the Prophet did okay, so I think I can bear it.' Or, you could go the other way; you could say, 'I'm not the Prophet! I can't handle this.' I find myself sometimes having those kinds of conversations with Allah!"

Likewise, when her husband died, one New Yorker was comforted to remember how the central figures of the Bahá'í Faith had grieved openly when they lost their loved ones. It gave her the assurance that it was okay to cry. "In the Bahá'í community," a businesswoman explains, "we pray for the progress of that person's soul. There are specific prayers we can say. We do whatever we can to shepherd that person's soul. We feel that prayer does have that impact. We are taught that the child can intercede on behalf of his or her deceased parents. I can pray for special consideration for my parents." That would seem to offer tremendous comfort. "It does indeed," she nods, "it does indeed. It is typical to feel a longing for the person who passed away. There are specific Bahá'í writings that talk about this, and describe the glorious next world that awaits us for the advancement of our soul. This is very attractive to Bahá'ís."

"After my father died, I continued to pray for him," a counselor recalls, "but I was experiencing a weird numbness. Then I got a phone call from one of the members of our National Spiritual Assembly who is also a psychologist. 'Yes, Bahá'u'lláh has said, *I have sent death as a messenger of joy to thee; wherefore dost thou grieve?* But,' he reminded me, '*that* Hidden Word is for the one who is passing. *We* are permitted to grieve!'"

"Cherokee see death as a natural process," Dawi Wistona explains, "but it is certainly a time for tremendous sadness. We believe that death should be respected, and that grieving should not be diminished. All too often, in the dominant culture, there is this sense of 'It's been three months; get over it.' But grief is not necessarily something somebody is going to get over in three months. Cherokee people are not all that emotive in public, but they are privately. It is common for people to go into a significant period of mourning, where they do not participate in ceremonies (except for personal ones). Then, slowly, we try to help them come out of it and rejoin the community."

"Traditional daily personal rituals can be a tremendous help when grieving," he says. "Traditionally, Cherokee pray twice a day: when the sun rises and sets. I encourage this. I always tell people, 'If you don't get up when the sun gets up, the sun is still rising somewhere. It's still okay to do it.' In those private times, we try to take the opportunity not only to give thanks for what we have, but to address and let go of those things that are getting in our way of being a good human life in that day." Not only does this help mourners avoid recrimination and guilt, he concludes, "it reminds everyone to treat every day as precious, to let the people know we care about them."

"The beauty of Buddhism," says a Zen priest, "is that the grieving process begins the minute you start to practice Buddhism—because you are reminded continually that you're dying. *You're* going to die, so don't be so surprised when *someone else* dies. Do not feel that you've been suddenly abandoned. Begin to let go of body and mind and possessions right now, because it is all slipping away. This is the fundamental active teaching of Buddhism."

"With all Buddhist ceremonies," he notes, "I see a common thread that helps us with the grieving process. They are designed so that you see destruction. You see loss right in front of you. You see sacrifice right in front of you. The ceremonies are designed so that you give up, give up, give up. You slough off—because that is what you have to do. You're always burning something; you're always burying something; you're always giving something away; you're always washing it off."

"I do a lot of grief work," says a Taoist master in New York. "Part of our modern society is the notion that we have to accept the loss. Taoism says, 'Yes, loved ones are gone; but they are always with you.' You feel connection, at the same time accepting that the physical aspect of that being is no longer there. That is very important grief work."

"You know," he continues, "Elisabeth Kübler-Ross was a natural Taoist in her findings. She just listened. She observed phenomena. This is very important grief work. The Taoist says, 'Grieve, by all means.' As a matter of fact, it was the Chinese custom until the 1900s that, when a parent died, the surviving child—even if he were the emperor—would observe a three-year mourning period. Why three years? Because, when you are born, it is three years before you are able to be independent from the mother's breast." By analogy, when one loses a parent, it will be three years before you are "weaned" once again.

Hindus often comment that their belief in reincarnation gives them the strength to progress from intense grief to acceptance. It is similar among Jains. "Jains believe that when you're born, the same minute it is written when you're going to die," a pediatrician notes. "Life and death is a process which is going to go on, depending on *karma*. There is comfort in that. It encourages acceptance instead of regret."

Yet, a Jain internist counters, "no matter how much we know that somebody is going to pass on, and that we're definitely going to die, to face that is difficult. When my father died, I felt very, very bad, and I was down for some time. But Jains believe that when someone has died, the soul has already taken life somewhere else in this universe. I just thought, 'Now, his soul is different and I am different.' That's what helped me. I still remember him, and I still feel bad that I lost him, but I remember him in a good way—the good times that I had. Putting the whole thing in the concept of time for the universe, I think that's what helps me."

"Jainism teaches us to not have so much attachment," a family physician adds, "but other factors tell you that this was your father or son or brother. There *is* that attachment; and there is also a medical reason for this death. Jainism teaches us that, just as we look at the *tirthankaras,* how they set examples of knowledge and wisdom, so we look at this particular person who just passed. If we take the positive from this person, it's going to help us understand something good about life, and maybe give us a little bit of good *karma.*"

As an antidote to remaining stuck in the stage of intense grief, Buddhists like to recount the famous tale of Kisagotami, a woman who had waited for years to have a child, only to have him die as a toddler. The Venerable Kondanna picks up the story: "Kisagotami had seen death before; but somehow, when it came to her, she could not accept it. So she carried the dead baby from one doctor to another. Everyone told her, 'He is dead!' At the end, she turned to the Buddha for medicine. What did the Buddha say to her? 'If you can bring me a mustard seed from a family that has not experienced the death of a child, a parent, a husband, or a friend, then I promise I will help you.' So she went from home to home, asking for mustard seeds. Everyone had mustard seeds, but the problem was that in each home, someone had died. She came back to Buddha and said, 'I understand.' She released the Buddha from his promise. And she released herself from her burden, too."

"It is clear that what the Jewish tradition has taught over many years is thoughtful and helpful," a Conservative rabbi believes. "When a parent dies, we grieve—by which I mean we perform the public rituals—for a year. For everyone else, it's a month. While it's true that other relationships are replaceable in a way that a parent is not, there is still tremendous loss."

For example, the children of a parent who has died might abstain from attending joyous occasions like weddings or concerts as a way of fulfilling the commandment to honor one's father and mother, a Talmud scholar explains. Daily recitation of the Mourner's *Kaddish* is a practice which emerged during the Middle Ages, she notes. Since it requires a *minyan,* most people go to a synagogue to do this. It is said at Morning and Evening Prayer for parents for eleven months; for other loved ones, just for thirty days. After that, it is said on the *Yahrzeit,* the anniversary.

Anniversaries

A year after the death of a loved one, the pain may still linger, but perhaps it is less intense. Grieving may have passed, but remembrance may well continue. "My father passed away twenty years ago," says a Bahá'í cancer surgeon. "I say prayers for his progress every single day of my life. In times of tests and difficulties, I know he is praying for me." Whether in an individual way or with formal ritual, many religions provide for marking the anniversary of loss.

Sikhs hold a first-anniversary memorial service as a conclusion of the grief process. As with the funeral, this observance features a complete reading of the *Guru Granth Sahib.* "The whole year has been done, and you have gotten accustomed to life without this person," a nurse explains. "Usually, at this gathering, we serve sweets. It's more of a celebration that we've been able to pass through this whole phase successfully."

Around the first anniversary of the person's death, a Mohawk family will hold a memorial service, at which they will talk to the deceased loved one. "They'll use a fire and tobacco to communicate with the dead, and they'll have a feast," a chief explains. "That's where they say to the deceased person, 'Now you have to leave; and we're going to stop now. We're not going to mourn you anymore.'" The end of mourning is certainly not the end of remembering, however. "Every year we have ceremonies for all the dead from the beginning of time," he notes. These are big, all-night affairs in the spring and fall, featuring lots of song and ritual. "We call these Ghost Dances."

In the Vodou tradition, "at a year and a day, or at a year plus a few months after someone dies, another ceremony has to be done," Dowoti Désir explains. "This is a ceremony of trying to get the deceased person to communicate with the living. In some Afro-Atlantic traditions, you're not considered dead and truly gone until family does certain things. Until the eldest son, the eldest daughter comes and takes care of these things—even if they don't get around to it for twenty years or more—the funeral rites are not complete. The deceased person is in a kind of limbo, still in transit. In my own experience, this is what led me to become initiated as a priest. It was clear that something had not been done for one of my ancestors that should have been done. This issue had been outstanding for at least four or five generations. The reason I was being visited and bombarded and pestered by the dead was because it was my head that had been chosen to clear this up."

Maintaining home-shrines is an important aspect of remembrance in the whole range of Afro-Atlantic traditions, Professor Désir explains. "Ancestral shrines should be kept near a place where there is water, and at the foundation of the house, in the back. In the Old Country, our ancestors would have been buried near the foundation of the house. Here, we can't do that, but we can symbolize that by placing their photos near the foundation. I make do by using the first floor of my house, toward the back. I also happen to have a sink there. So that's where the shrine is. People who were important to us, we'll keep their image someplace, but we don't mingle the images of the living with the images of the dead. They have to have their separate spaces. As much as you love these people, as much as you miss them, it's got to be clear to them that our space is not theirs now."

"On the other hand," she stresses, "it is important that we keep uttering the names of those who came before us. It's a form of love, it's a form of homage, it's a form of acknowledging who we are as a person—how the wisdom, the mistakes, the trials and tribulations of those who came before us (and before them, and before them) have all helped define who we are in the here and the now."

The Theravada tradition includes the custom of all-night chanting on the anniversary of someone's death, or in remembrance of all family members who have passed away. "Some people are very fond of that," says the Venerable Kondanna, the abbot of the Staten Island Buddhist Vihara. "My family always does it between October and December, because my mother died in October and my father died in December." Traditionally, several monks would be present, as well as the extended family of the person who has requested the ceremony.

Japanese Pure Land Buddhists hold a memorial one hundred days after someone's death, and again at the end of the first year, the Reverend T. Kenjitsu Nakagaki explains. "There will be the Third Year memorial service, which is actually after two years; then the Seventh Year memorial service; then the Thirteenth Year memorial." Some families hold memorials on the seventeenth, twenty-third, and twenty-seventh years; some also mark the twenty-fifth. "The Thirty-Three Year memorial is normally a big one; then, the Fiftieth Year memorial; and that's about it"—presumably, because at that point there would be only a few people who would remember this person.

Are these memorial services sad occasions? Joyous occasions? The clue is in the name: *Shotsuki Hoyo,* Joyous Month Service. "Traditionally, these are occasions when the whole family gathers," he says. "In a way, it's good, because other people are sharing in the sadness—in the beginning part. Later on, after the Thirteenth Year's gathering, they change the focus. Remembering the loved one's death brings the family together, so it is a happy occasion." In a large family, these memorials would be happening all the time; the family would be marking different stages for various deceased loved ones. And, if these persons died on the Buddha's path, he notes, their status has changed: "They become *bodhisattvas* who guide the rest of us."

"Chinese society has integrated death as part of life," this master reminds us. "Once a year there is a festival in April called *Ching Ming,* the Day of the Dead. We converge in the cemetery for a big picnic. Celebrating the Day of the Dead may seem macabre, but it is life! You have to make a transition to a different relationship, one that has passed from the physical plane. That's why you can have a picnic in a cemetery. We do the same thing we do after a funeral. We have a picnic next to the gravesite."

Chinese cemetery customs have been adapted to the American context. When one visits the grave of a family member, it is customary to leave food for "hungry ghosts" (ancestors whose souls carried so much negative baggage that they have fallen into the realm of torment). One may leave any other items the departed might need for their journey to Heaven: oranges, bottles of beer or soda, incense, tea—even chopsticks. For Taoists, these practices not only relieve the hunger and thirst of the dead, but also transform their negative energy so as to free them from spiritual suffering and hasten their ascent out of the Hungry Ghost Realm.

"For Hindus, the ceremony performed on the first anniversary of someone's death is called the *shraddha,* remembrance," a professor explains. "People do different kinds of rituals to honor the deceased. In a Vedic sense, they pay rent in heaven: they do various propitiatory rituals that maintain a deceased person's status in heaven." This is a holdover from earlier notions of what happens when we die, he explains. Notions of *samsara,* reincarnation, and *moksha* come from the *Upanishads,* literature that is much more recent than the Vedas. *Shraddha* is a Vedic ritual in which *svaga,* heaven, is key.

"You are supposed to go to the Ganges River and do the first *shraddha* there," an engineer explains. "There is specific month allocated for these things. It is the same month for everybody. Suppose your parents passed away on the fifth day of the month. Then within this month for *shraddha,* you would honor them on the fifth day. You put some donation in the temple; then you feed a holy man, and your grandkids or relatives. Every year it happens. It's part of the grieving process. Not only that, the belief is that if you do these things, their soul will benefit. This is how we remember."

On the first anniversary of the cremation, the relatives of one Hindu woman traveled from Ohio to India to perform *shraddha* and to deposit her ashes in the Ganges River. The family had kept the ashes at home until this point. "That's not usual," her nephew notes. "It's interesting that Hindus in America are willing to do some things here, but then they still want to go back to India for the ceremony to become 'official.'" Thinking back on Hindu notions of personhood, he suggests that, for many Hindus in America, "there is a sense of 'de-personhood' that can only be established in India, in a way. Sometimes it involves going to the Ganges River and depositing the ashes. For American Hindus, you would think that the Cuyahoga or the Mississippi River would be sufficient, but it is not."

Zoroastrians hold special prayers for the deceased once a month for six months, and then at the end of the first year. Many families hold an annual memorial as well, which usually takes the form of *Jashan,* a formal worship rite that can be performed for any festival or memorial occasion. Only the prayers change, depending on the intent of the ceremony. At a memorial *Jashan,* a young medical student explains, "You are praying that his or her soul is being taken care of. So, you're not forgetting about the person, and you are hoping they are in a good place."

"All Zoroastrian ceremonies are done in the presence of fire—the symbol of Ahura Mazda and his spirit of righteousness," a New Jersey priest explains. During *Jashan,* a fire is lit in an urn, which the priest tends throughout the ritual, wearing white clothing and a mask, so as not to pollute the flames. The flames rise and ebb as he adds more incense—small pieces of sandalwood. All of the elements of creation are represented on the platform where the priest sits: fruit and flowers, representing the plant kingdom; milk (or even a goldfish swimming in a bowl) representing the animal kingdom; and metal, representing the earth. Fire, as the most powerful of cleansing agents, represents purity; and the priest himself represents humanity.

In addition to family memorials, "we Zoroastrians also have a time of the year when we pay respect to all departed souls," the medical student adds. "It is the last five days of our calendar year, before we start a new year." Parsis call this *Muktad* Days; for Iranians, it is *Panjeh*. "And some call this *Gatha* Days, because the *Gathas* are scriptures that Zarathustra wrote, and there are five of them. Each of the five days, a different *Gatha* is recited by the priest. People will bring flowers or whatever. It is almost like an offering to the departed as well. It's not 'mourning'; it's remembrance: you are remembering the deceased, and you are wishing their souls well."

"I remember that when I was a teenager," says Dr. Kersey Antia, "if a person died during the *Muktad,* the family would not observe the *Muktad* ceremony for other deceased relatives, presumably because the *fravashis* were busy helping this recently departed soul. There are variations on this custom, but its implication is clear, and our scriptures tell us: the souls of our departed relatives do come to greet us and instruct us in the ways of the other world." The scriptures say that departed souls crave our attention, he notes. One passage says, "Who will praise us? Who will venerate us? Who will show love for us?" For this reason, Dr. Antia explains, "it is not surprising that our third most important prayer relates to the veneration of all worthy souls, and that the scriptures also exhort us to hold proper rituals in memory of departed souls and to venerate them collectively at the end of the year."

In the Jewish tradition, on the anniversary of the death of a parent or close relative, it is the custom to light a *Yahrzeit* candle, which burns for twenty-four hours, and to visit the cemetery. "When we visit a grave," an educator explains, "we leave a stone on top of the gravestone. You almost *never* see flowers. You do absolutely see stones. Definitely, some Jews pray at a gravesite, and there are definitely Jews who are very much against this. They think it might be confused with the praying *to* the person who has died, when one's prayers should be directed to God only." Beyond these family customs, the full community remembers its dead ritually by reciting the *yizkor,* the remembrance prayer, each year on *Yom Kippur, Passover, Shavuot,* and *Sukkot.*

"The idea of putting mourning into a time-frame tends to be reassuring to people," says the leader of a Jewish congregation. "They can talk to people who have been through that process and see that things do change. Also, when things are changing, you can feel normal about that. You see that you are supposed to progress. It is okay for you to be less sad as time goes on." Whatever their religion, most people would agree!

When Loss Is Multireligious

We have seen how valuable it can be when our religion provides a regimen for sitting with loss and celebrating memory. Whatever their religion, some family members will be more observant than others. Questions arise. To what extent, for example, should the sensibilities of the most observant be accommodated? Some American families are multireligious. To what extent may nonadherents of a religion participate in its funeral and mourning rituals? When we look beyond our own family and into the neighborhood itself, we are well aware that the attacks on September 11, 2001, and Hurricane Katrina gave Americans experience with multireligious loss on a large scale. "Disasters do not respect religious traditions and practices," says one expert in disaster spiritual care. In mass mortality situations, she emphasizes, "we are not able to do Buddhist things for Buddhist victims, and Muslim things for Muslim victims—not because people are insensitive, but just because that is the nature of the situation." Yet the tapestry of America's many religious traditions and practices still needs to be respected, and in fact plays an important role in healing.

9/11
In the aftermath of the September 11 attacks, multireligious memorial events, such as a prayer service in Yankee Stadium, provided vehicles for expressing grief and solidarity while honoring the dead. "A community prayer service is an effort to turn toward the existential or transcendent dimension of our religion in an attempt to understand what happened," says Steve

Spreitzer, executive director of the Michigan Roundtable for Diversity and Inclusion. Its affiliate, Interfaith Partners, sponsored a memorial service in the Detroit area soon after 9/11 and a Caravan of Remembrance one year later. "From the beginning, however," he stresses, "we wanted to move beyond prayers and holding hands. Very quickly, we went from memorializing to projects like building something together."

When loss is multireligious, "holding hands and praying" and "building something" multireligiously do have value. But so do the things religion-communities do individually on behalf of the whole. This is *pragmatic pluralism,* says Laurie Patton of Emory University. "There are moments when one religion needs another to be itself; occasions when difference is needed—not tolerated, not dialogued about, but needed—because our survival depends upon it." In the wake of the attacks on the World Trade Center, there were many attempts at spiritual care proffered by one religious tradition for the betterment of everyone.

For example, upon learning of the attacks, a priest in Washington State performed Shinto rituals of purification. A Hare Krishna monk drove from West Virginia to New York City, chose a spot in the northwest corner of Union Square Park, and chanted there for five days, his pleasant tenor voice wafting above traffic noise and pedestrian scuffling. Why had he come? "We believe that chant changes what is possible for God to accomplish," he explained. "We chant to help create new possibilities in the world." Orthodox Jews organized themselves to perform the *mitzvah* of *shmirah,* the act of guarding the dead from the moment of passing until they are buried. Under normal circumstances, this ritual recitation of psalms would be performed for twenty-four hours at most. But in this extraordinary situation, it was maintained for many weeks next to the morgue and its adjunct refrigerator trucks full of body parts. Since the Orthodox do not travel on the Sabbath, students from Stern College for Women, whose dormitory was near the morgue, took responsibility for that twenty-five-hour period each week. Thus vigil was kept for all these human remains—Jewish or not.

Horrified by the ugliness perpetrated in the name of their religion, many Muslims sought ways to show Americans another face of Islam. In late September 2001, one Muslim couple walked to the church nearest their Brooklyn apartment and invited the entire congregation to stop by their home for lemonade and cookies after Sunday worship. Many accepted. Recalling how the Prophet Muhammad had said that "God is beautiful and he loves beauty," the American Society for Muslim Advancement (ASMA) sponsored *Reflections at a Time of Transformation,* an event featuring Muslim painters, photographers, calligraphers, musicians, and poets, presented in early 2002 as a gift of beauty to a wounded city.

His Holiness the Dalai Lama led a gathering in prayer and instruction at Ground Zero, and in mid-December 2001 sent a team of twenty monks to construct a 7-foot-by-7-foot *mandala* of Yamantaka (Terminator of Death) out of colored sand in a museum near the ruins of the World Trade Center. Its unusually large size was meant to echo the immensity of the assault and the vastness of the need for healing. The monks then repeated the task near the Pentagon. A completed sand *mandala* is consecrated by a ritual much like the one that began the process, then it is deconstructed ritually. All of the sand is swept up. Some of it is given to onlookers as a blessing; the rest is collected, carried in an urn to the nearby river, then poured into the water so that the current might distribute the healing energy to the entire world. "This is one of the greatest things we have to learn," a layman reminds us: "that life is impermanent; life leads inevitably to death. That's one reason why the monks make these beautiful images, then brush up the sand and pour it into the river. The sand *mandala* is impermanent; and we're impermanent. It brings us back to the very foundations of our practice."

Hindus arranged for a *pujari* to sprinkle some Ganges water on Ground Zero. Identifying the deceased is part of the cremation ceremony, a devotee explains. In Hindu understanding, the human body is composed of the *pancha mahabhuta,* the five elements of earth, fire, wind, water, and ether. "At Ground Zero, we had the ashes of hundreds and hundreds of people whose deaths had occurred in such an extremely violent way. Quite obviously, the *pancha mahabhuta* of many hundreds of people were being breathed in, but there was no way to identify exactly *whose* elements. At least, we Hindus believed, by means of this ceremony some sanctifying would take place."

Every year since 2002, the New York Buddhist Church—a Pure Land temple—has held a Floating Lantern ceremony in memory of the victims of the 9/11 attacks. While the Japanese community hosts the event, representatives of many forms of Buddhist and many other religions also participate. The large crowd gathers at a pier on the Hudson River, north of Ground Zero, for a ceremony of music, official messages, meditation, prayer, and chanting. Anyone may write the name of a deceased loved one or a message for peace on paper lanterns that will be attached to little "rafts." Trains of lanterns are lit as the sun sets, launched in the Hudson River, then pulled away from the pier by members of the New York Kayak Company. "As we pay respect for lives lost at the World Trade Center," says the Reverend T. Kenjitsu Nakagaki, "we offer the light of hope for a peaceful world and the end of suffering."

In an urban disaster situation, the multireligious nature of the loss adds layers of complexity to offering hope and alleviating suffering—spiritual as well as physical. Peter Gudaitis, executive director of New York Disaster Interfaith Services, is well known for the guidance and instruction he has provided, not only to New York City, but also to other cities in the United States and Europe. He believes that disaster spiritual care is something that all faith communities should have the opportunity to provide. Disaster victims deserve care that is grounded in their own beliefs and sources of strength with regard to the sacred. They should also be protected from opportunists who take advantage of vulnerability in times of crisis to promote their own faith or agenda. Therefore, Peter advocates that just as medical caregivers must have specialized training and licensing to perform certain services, so should religious leaders or chaplains be trained in the specific skills necessary for providing disaster spiritual care that is emotionally healthy and theologically sound.

Hurricane Katrina

"Hurricane Katrina struck on the birthday of Lord Krishna," explains a member of the Hindu Temple of Greater New Orleans. "We had planned to hold a celebration, and we had to postpone everything. We said, 'God willing, we'll do it next year.'" As with the September 11 attacks, the losses occasioned by Hurricane Katrina were also profoundly multireligious. Victims and evacuees included thousands of Christians, but also Buddhists, Bahá'ís, Jains, Hindus, Muslims, Jews, Vodouisants, and Sikhs.

Body-recovery and mortuary services in Katrina's aftermath were provided by a private corporation contracted by the U.S. government with orders to hire chaplains to accompany its recovery teams. This was unusual. Military chaplains hold military rank, but they are not selected directly by a government agency; their faith-communities determine whether they serve. With Katrina, it seems that a government-mandated agency actually went out and hired clergy. Whenever a body was located, recovery-team members were to pause, remove their hats, and bow their heads. The team chaplain's short prayer would offer thanks for the deceased person's life and for the workers who had found the corpse. For many it seemed like a reverent gesture to have chaplains accompanying the body-retrieval teams, but for others it raised ethical questions as to whom the clergy were responsible and under whose authority they were conducting sacred services.

Many hundreds of churches were damaged or destroyed by Katrina and its aftermath, but so were synagogues, mosques, *gurdwaras, mandirs,* temples, *péristyles, zendos,* and yoga centers. New Orleans's Sri Veera Venkata Satyanarayana Hindu Temple sustained serious wind damage, but suffered more from looting. "Many of the silver objects used during *puja* were stolen," a graduate student explains.

We have learned how religions' rituals, practices, and ceremonies sustain people in the face of loss, and carry them through the stages of grieving. Since these rituals often require special objects and specialized space, it is small wonder, then, that religion-communities affected by the megastorm of August 2005 demonstrated immediate deep concern for the safety of sacred statues and scriptures. In itself this was a form of "pragmatic pluralism": an effort to conserve the region's multireligiousness itself.

All Vietnamese Buddhist temples along the Gulf Coast of Alabama and Mississippi were damaged, so congregations in Bayou La Batre and Biloxi were relieved to discover that somehow their statues of Shakyamuni and Quan Am had survived the onslaught. Hare Krishnas drove a huge truck into flooded New Orleans to collect their temple's deity-images and transport them to safety in Dallas. The U.S. chapter of United Sikhs arranged for a dramatic helicopter rescue of the copy of the *Guru Granth Sahib* (scriptures—honored as a living teacher) from the New Orleans Gurdwara Sahib, a temple serving families from all over Louisiana as well as parts of Florida, Alabama, and Mississippi.

Rosh ha-Shanah, the Jewish New Year, came quickly after the disaster. Since the Orthodox synagogue was underwater, that congregation went to an undamaged Conservative synagogue to celebrate the High Holy Days. They were grateful to be able to worship, a rabbi explains, but the differences between Conservative and Orthodox styles of worship made them even more aware of their loss. So where could a temporary Orthodox synagogue be created? Help came from a non-Jewish Korean-American who offered a worship space in his hotel, and—since observant Jews do not travel during *Shabbat*—Friday night accommodations in his hotel for all the members of the congregation, so they would be where they needed to be for as many Sabbaths as necessary. Help also came in the form of a gift of a Torah scroll—which, along with an ark to store it in and a *Ner Tamid* (eternal light), define a space as a synagogue. In the days following the flood, some forty Torah scrolls were rescued from the hurricane region. The following March, scrolls that were too badly damaged were given a ceremonial burial.

As we have seen, one way that religions facilitate the grieving process is through their teachings on and methods for caring for those who have suffered loss. So, in addition to addressing their own immediate concerns, many faith-groups—including the Tzu Chi Foundation (a Taiwanese Buddhist organization), United Sikhs, BAPS (Hindu devotees of Swaminarayan),

Mississippi's Vietnamese Buddhist community, some two thousand members of Houston's Muslim community, and the nascent Texas Muslim Women's Foundation—worked parallel to or in partnership with Christian and secular relief organizations to provide help to whomever needed it, dispensing emotional, psychological, and material help along with food, shelter, and supplies. Hindu communities from around the United States sent teams to help with clean-up and rebuilding—many of them teens and college students, many of them working with Habitat for Humanity. The Islamic Circle of North America (ICNA), a national organization, took a holistic approach. An ICNA family would take responsibility for an evacuee-family, matching needs with resources on a case-by-case basis.

The Jewish community of Baton Rouge played a major role in accounting for missing members of New Orleans synagogues and contacting the loved ones of victims and evacuees, a rabbi notes. "One synagogue administrator said she knew the emergency was over when people stopped calling her on Saturdays— when *Shabbat* was *Shabbat* again!"

Once the Louisiana Jewish community was ready to move from emergency mode to recovery of a different sort, officers of the National Jewish Center for Learning and Leadership arrived to lead workshops. "We began with a lesson from the Book of Job," Rabbi Tzvi Blanchard explains. "Job teaches that sometimes answers are not what you're looking for. We have to accept the fact that we don't understand these things. Next, we took a piece from Ecclesiastes which says there is a wheel of life: things do go down, but they also start coming back up. We asked: Do you see any signs, little signs? We let people talk for two hours, telling stories about little signs of coming back up."

"Then," he continues, "we talked about what the Rabbis did in the face of the loss of the Temple in 70 CE. Their strategy was to reassert the primacy of the everyday, the holiness and sanctity of the everyday, and to frame response to loss in terms of holiness. We went over the blessings the Rabbis laid out for us to do. We asked these Katrina victims what they would say blessings for. Their list was amazing. One person said she would say a blessing over the fact that last night, for the first time since Katrina, the family ate dinner together in their house—

although they had to do it on the second floor since the first level is gone. Indeed, the strategies of the Rabbis can serve us well, whatever form loss takes."

Shortly after Hurricane Katrina's onslaught, the Reverend Jennie Thomas, pastoral care coordinator and chaplain at Ochsner Clinic Foundation in New Orleans, made a national appeal for prayers she could circulate to Ochsner's staff by email each day. For about two months, prayers flowed in regularly, which she then passed along to all employees. Many of the prayers were Christian, but there were also some Jewish prayers, a Buddhist meditation, and some prayers she describes as interfaith. "People went out of their way to thank me for putting those prayers on email," she recalls. "It helped to know that others were praying as we recovered from this disaster."

Reflections

While spiritual care was provided and faith-based action was taken by people of many religions, the efforts described here probably have been negligible factors in the overall ongoing restoration of New Orleans, surmises Professor Timothy Cahill of Loyola University New Orleans. Some would hold a similar assessment of the role the various religion-communities have played during the months following 9/11. On the other hand, many people would argue that all of these efforts have value, no matter how small or insignificant they may seem. "One of the things Katrina has shown us, and definitely my work as a Buddhist chaplain affirms this," asserts the Reverend David Zuniga, "is that, in working with the end of life, you can see the absolute best of human nature. You see people who are brave, who have humor and grace amidst a tremendous amount of suffering; you also see the very worst in human behavior. All things are interconnected, and Katrina provides a very skillful lens through which to see this in order to learn spiritual lessons."

In this book we have seen how the religions of our neighbors reveal that all losses—not just those caused by disaster or violence—can indeed be a "lens" through which we can "learn spiritual lessons." For, while the title of this book is *Loss,* it has also been about recovery. We have heard how the rituals and practices of many different religion-communities help their members to overcome the sting of the loss and to restore a healthful routine. We have discovered how our neighbors of various faiths understand destiny; how they perceive meaning and assign value—a core characteristic of personhood; how they experience the grace of ritual and the graciousness of concern. We have seen how they embrace the notion of a "good death"—a death which is dignified, facilitated with ritual, and memorialized.

This book has also been about the many ways our neighbors' religions help them access the spiritual resources we all need in times of loss. We have seen our neighbors guided by sacred texts and traditions in making difficult healthcare decisions, and finding joy and peace in spiritual care—as givers and as recipients. They have found solace in chant and storytelling, but also in silence. Their religious traditions have strengthened them to face change and to make change. In these and in countless other ways, faith in its many forms enriches America's neighborhoods.

Resources

QUICK INFORMATION GUIDE TO RELIGIONS

The descriptions below are meant to give the reader with little or no background knowledge of the world's religions a *very* rudimentary orientation to the origins, beliefs, and practices of the religions discussed in *Faith in the Neighborhood*.

Afro-Caribbean Religion

Afro-Caribbean religion is an umbrella term for adaptations of African traditional religion brought to the Western hemisphere during the Middle Passage (the era of slave-trading), including Vodou (Afro-Haitian religion) and Lùkùmì (Afro-Cuban religion, also called Santería). Sacred knowledge is conveyed by means of storytelling and sung narratives, which may exist in written form but not in the sense of a "holy book" equivalent to the Bible for Christians. Believers seek divine guidance from many sources.

Beliefs: The One Supreme God is believed to be manifested through spirits (called *lwa* in Vodou, or *orisha* in Lùkùmì) and ancestors. Sacred energies reaffirm each individual's ties to the spiritual realm, to ancestors, and to the community.

Practices: Autonomous practice-groups (called families) are formed through initiation. The initiates of a particular priest are his or her "children." Priests (women or men) perform rituals and healing exercises.

To dig deeper: Fernandez-Olmos, Margarite, and Lizabeth Paravisini-Gebert. *Creole Religions of the Caribbean: An Introduction from Vodou and Santeria to Obeah and Espiritismo.* New York: New York University Press, 2003.

Bahá'í

The Bahá'í Faith was founded in mid-nineteenth-century Iran by Mírzá Husayn-Alí Núrí, called Bahá'u'lláh by followers. Shoghi Effendi Rabbani (Bahá'u'lláh's grandson) established the Bahá'í administrative order and supervised the faith's spread worldwide. The writings of Bahá'u'lláh (more than one hundred volumes) form the core of Bahá'í scripture. The writings of 'Abdu'l-Bahá (Bahá'u'lláh's son and interpreter) and Shoghi Effendi (his grandson) also have special status. Bahá'ís revere and use the sacred texts of the world's other religions as well.

Beliefs: According to its doctrine of progressive revelation, the Bahá'í Faith is the fulfillment of all prior religions, and provides divine guidance for this age. Bahá'u'lláh and his herald, the Báb (Sayyid 'Ali Muhammad), are revered as the Twin Manifestations of God who proclaimed God's message for the present age: the oneness of God, the oneness of religion, and the oneness of humankind. The Bahá'í Faith champions racial and gender equality, economic justice, universal education, ecological sensitivity, the essential harmony of science and religion, and the establishment of a universal language and a world federal system.

Practices: The Bahá'í Faith has clearly defined local, national, and international administrative principles, with all decision-making by consultation and consensus. A local assembly requires a quorum of nine members. There are no ordained clergy, and little in the way of prescribed rituals. Members are encouraged to pray, meditate, and read from the Bahá'í writings daily. They are obligated to practice chastity and monogamy, and to abstain from alcohol and drugs. They meet regularly in a home or community center for worship, consultation, and fellowship at the beginning of each of the nineteen months of the Bahá'í calendar. A fast is observed annually from March 2 to March 20.

To dig deeper: Momen, Moojan. *The Bahá'í Faith: A Short Introduction.* Oxford: Oneworld, 1997.

Buddhism

Buddhism is a Western term for the many expressions of the teachings of the Buddha, Siddhartha Gautama (c. 563–483 BCE), who rejected the extremes of excessive self-indulgence and rigorous asceticism for a Middle Way of morality, concentration, and wisdom. Theravada (Way of the Elders), the southern branch, is dominant in Sri Lanka and most of mainland Southeast Asia. Mahayana (Great Vehicle), the northern branch, took root in China, Tibet, Viet Nam, Korea, and Japan, and includes schools such as Pure Land, Nichiren, and Zen. Vajrayana (Diamond Vehicle), which emphasizes compassionate action and special practices under the guidance of a teacher, is considered a form of Mahayana by some scholars, and a distinct western branch by others. It is associated primarily (although not exclusively) with Tibet, but not all Tibetan Buddhists practice Vajrayana. All of the above are present in the United States, and a distinct and eclectic American Buddhism is emerging as well. A vast body of ancient authoritative literature is believed to be definitive records of the teachings of the Buddha himself, but no single collection of writings is revered by all Buddhists. Individual sects have generated authoritative literature in their own right up to the present time. Most American temples and practice-groups are autonomous.

Beliefs: The Buddha taught Four Noble Truths: that life inevitably involves suffering; that the origin of suffering is desire; that suffering will end when desire is extinguished; and, that desire is extinguished by following the Noble Eightfold Path (right understanding, thought, speech, action, livelihood, effort, mindfulness, and meditation). This will lead to achievement of Nirvana (cessation of participation in *samsara,* the endless cycle of birth, death, and rebirth). The Mahayana ideal is the *bodhisattva*—one who attains Nirvana but refuses it, remaining in *samsara* in order to bring others to enlightenment. Traditionally, Buddhists "take refuge" in the Buddha, the *Dharma* (teachings), and the *Sangha* (community), but may differ in their interpretation of these terms.

Practice: All forms of Buddhism emphasize mindfulness—being fully present in whatever one is doing. Monasticism has a significant place in most forms of Buddhism, but lay and monastic roles are less differentiated in Mahayana. Daily devotional practice varies from branch to branch, but may include meditation, selfless service, paying respect to others, study, or chanting.

To dig deeper: Snelling, John. *The Buddhist Handbook: A Complete Guide to Buddhist Schools, Teaching, Practice, and History,* revised and updated. Rochester, Vt.: Inner Traditions International, 1999.

Confucianism

Confucianism refers to those beliefs and practices based on the socio-political teachings of K'ung Fu-tse (Master Kung). He lived in China, 551–479 BCE, and promulgated *Ju-Chiao* (the teachings of the scholars). Major texts are the *Analects* of K'ung Fu-tse, the *Doctrine of the Mean,* the *Great Learning,* and the writing of Mencius. Confucianism was the state religion of during several eras of China's history.

Beliefs: Confucianism seeks to create true spiritual nobility by developing the virtues. Its core concept is the importance of harmony in the family, the community, and the state. In Confucian understanding, the Tao is the way human beings should follow. As some Confucians see it, "Heaven" is the ethical principle of orderliness; for others, "Heaven" is "Lord on High" (akin to God-as-personal).

Practice: Veneration of ancestors and deities, worship of Heaven, development of the virtues, and maintenance of essential societal relationships are to be done with attention to propriety and detail. Festivals are celebrated according to a lunar calendar, adjusted periodically to the solar agricultural seasons. Confucianism has long been practiced in conjunction with Taoism and Mahayana Buddhism as the Three Teachings.

To dig deeper: Jochim, Christian. *Chinese Religions: A Cultural Perspective.* Englewood Cliffs, N.J.: Prentice-Hall, 1986.

Hinduism

Hinduism is a Western label for *Sanatana Dharma* (Eternal Law), and is an umbrella term for a number of streams of beliefs and practices with roots in the Indian subcontinent. It has a vast heritage of sacred texts, including the Vedas, the *Upanishads,* and epics like the *Ramayana* and *Mahabharata.* However, no specific ones are authoritative for all Hindus everywhere. The *Bhagavad-Gita* (Song of God) is a well-known portion of the *Mahabharata.* In addition to the ancient classic literature, some congregations give particular priority to the writings of their own current or founding spiritual leader.

Beliefs: In general, Hindus believe in Brahman: one Ultimate Reality—both ever-present and beyond time and space. Brahman is both impersonal and personal. Some understand Brahman-as-Personal is Vishnu; for others, it is Shiva. For still others, it is the Divine Mother (the Parashakti, called by various names such as Durga or Kali or Parvati). Others understand all of Hinduism's many deities as pointers to particular aspects, powers, and functions of the one Ultimate Reality. Hinduism teaches *samsara,* an endless cycle of birth, death, and rebirth that causes each soul to transmigrate from one earthly existence to another and to progress toward maturity and achievement of *moksha* (release and return to Ultimate Reality). Hindus believe in *karma*—the moral and physical law of cause and effect. Following *Dharma* (divine law) brings one into harmony with Ultimate Reality. Some streams of Hinduism are monistic, teaching that the Ultimate Creator and all creatures are of the same substance.

Practice: Some Hindus are devotees of a particular deity and may consider themselves to belong to one of the three main subtraditions of Hinduism: Shaivites (devotees of Shiva), Vaishnavites (devotees of Vishnu), and Shaktas (devotees the Divine Mother). Devotees of a particular guru (teacher and spiritual leader) may be identified by the name of the movement he or she founded. Hindu yoga (spiritual discipline) takes many forms: *karma yoga,* the path of selfless action; *raja yoga,* meditation or psychological exercises; *hatha yoga,* postures and breathing exercises; and *jnana yoga,* study. *Bhakti yoga* (devotional activities performed at a home or community shrine) includes *darshan* (seeing and being seen by holy images or people), *puja* (ritual offering to the deity), *abhishekam* (bathing a sacred image), *yajna* (fire sacrifice), or pilgrimage. Holidays are observed by *puja*, festivals, fasts, dance, chant, and readings or dramatizations of sacred texts.

To dig deeper: Narayanan, Vasudha. *Hinduism: Origins, Beliefs, Practices, Holy Texts, Sacred Places.* New York: Oxford, 2004.

Islam

Islam is based on divine revelations received by the Prophet Muhammad (570–632 CE) in the Arabia peninsula, 610–632 CE. For Muslims, the Qur'an, Islam's holy book, contains the very words of God, summarizing and superceding previous scriptures. Second in authority is the Prophet's *Sunnah* (his example—his own sayings and deeds), authenticated and compiled as the huge body of literature called the *Hadith* (report, tradition). Islam also has a vast legacy of literature on Islamic law, philosophy, theology, and mysticism. Islam's two major branches, Sunni and Shi'ah, agree on most matters of doctrine and practice, but differ on issues of authority. Sufism, whose adherents may come from either branch, denotes a broad range of belief and practice focusing on Islam's mystical dimension. Since the mid-1960s, most African-American Muslims have been Sunni Muslims, but a few are Shi'ah, and others belong to movements such as the Nation of Islam that differ sharply from the mainstream in belief and practice.

Beliefs: Muslims believe that there is but One God, whom they call by the Arabic word Allah. God is unique and incomparable, but can be described in terms of attributes, such as "the Merciful" and "the Compassionate." God has created all that is, and has complete authority over human destiny. On the Day of Judgment everyone will be called to account. Spiritual heritage is traced to Abraham through his son Ishmael. The Ka'aba (the ancient shrine toward which all Muslim prayer is oriented) is said to have been erected by Adam and restored by Abraham, Islam's spiritual ancestor. Muslims believe God has sent many prophets, including Abraham, Moses, and Jesus, but that Muhammad is the "Seal," the last in this chain.

Practices: Islam has Five Pillars of obligatory practice: ritual testimony to God's oneness and Muhammad's messengerhood, ritual prayer five times a day, annual return of a percentage of one's wealth to the community, fasting during the month of Ramadan; and pilgrimage to the holy city of Mecca (health and means permitting). *Jum'ah* (congregational worship) is held on Fridays in the early afternoon. The Islamic calendar is lunar, and holidays shift through the solar seasons.

All Muslims believe in *Shari'ah* (divine law), the primary sources for which are the Qur'an and the Prophet's *Sunnah.* The sciences of Qur'an commentary and Islamic jurisprudence *(fiqh)*—of which there have always been multiple schools of interpretation—are the means by which divine revelation is applied to daily life. Islamic legal reasoning defines what Islam considers *halal* (permissible) and *haram* (prohibited) in all aspects of life.

To dig deeper: Elias, Jamal J. *Islam.* Upper Saddle River, N.J.: Prentice-Hall, 1999.

Jainism

Jainism (from the Sanskrit *jina*—"conqueror" of one's inner passions) is an ancient Indian religion based on the notion that the cosmos goes through unceasing six-hundred-million-year cycles of integration and disintegration. With each eon of disintegration comes a series of twenty-four *tirthankaras* (crossing-makers)—great spiritual leaders who attain infinite knowledge, revive the Jain way of life, establish a monastic order, and assist in the liberation of countless other human beings. Mahavira (599–527 BCE) was the twenty-fourth and last *tirthankara* for the current eon. His sermons provide the core of Jain scriptures, the *Agam Sutras,* but Jainism's two branches differ over the exact contents. Each branch also supplements this with scholarly works dating from the first ten centuries of the common era.

Beliefs: Jains believe that the universe is beginningless and endless. Nothing is ever created or destroyed. Everything undergoes continuous self-modification, without a divine manager. Jainism teaches that *perfect being*—pure consciousness with no *karma* attached to it—is attainable by all. Human beings who have rid themselves of all *karmas* break free of the wheel of *samsara* (worldly concerns) and become liberated, omniscient, omnipotent souls.

Practices: Jainism promotes religious tolerance, ethical purity, environmental harmony, and spiritual contentment. Its core principles are *ahimsa* (non-harming), *anekantwad* (non-onesidedness), and *aparigraha* (non-attachment). It advocates a life directed by right knowledge, right faith, and right conduct. Dedicated Jains take five vows: non-violence, truthfulness, non-stealing, celibacy, and non-attachment. Asceticism is the ideal. Jain monks or nuns take rigorous vows, and some laypersons take on an eleven-stage discipline of increasing renunciation. Jains practice strict vegetarianism, and many maintain a rhythm of regular fasting. Many (but not all) Jains employ images of one or more of the *tirthankaras* in their devotional practice.

To dig deeper: Tobias, Michael. *Life Force: The World of Jainism.* Fremont, Calif.: Jain Publishing, 1991.

Judaism

Judaism is founded on the ancient Middle Eastern monotheistic religion of the people of Israel and their ritual practice, which came to be centered in the temple in Jerusalem. Traditionally, Jews are defined as a people in relationship with the one and only Creator who established a covenant relationship with the patriarch Abraham, who spoke to humanity through Moses on Mount Sinai, and who gave a series of commandments by which this covenant people is to live. Judaism now refers to the system of beliefs and practices developed after the destruction of the temple by the Romans in 70 CE. In place of temple sacrifice, Jews now are to engage in prayer, repentance, and *tzedakah* (giving of charity and striving for justice). Present-day Jews share a sense of peoplehood—a sense of history that includes exodus from slavery, receipt of a homeland designated by God, destruction of the homeland, diaspora, Holocaust, and return to the homeland by establishment of the modern state of Israel.

Beliefs and Practices: The home is central to practice. While the synagogue (from the Greek for "a gathering") is central to community life, some Jews choose to join a *chavurah* (friendship group), a *minyan* (prayer quorum), or a Jewish philanthropic or advocacy organization instead of—or in addition to—synagogue membership. During the twentieth century, American Judaism diverged into various philosophical and liturgical movements differing on interpretation of Torah and Talmud, thus in degree and style of practice—especially regarding rules of eating, dress, and Sabbath observance.

Orthodox refers to various current expressions (ranging from ultra-traditional to Hassidic to modern) of pre-Enlightenment traditional Judaism, all of which accept the divine authorship of the Torah, and the divine, binding, unchangeable nature of *Halakhah* (Jewish law). *Reform* sees the Torah and Talmud as divinely inspired, but humanly recorded. Observance is a matter of informed individual choice. Greater emphasis is put on ethics and social action than on ritual. Modernization of Jewish rituals and practices and broad use of the vernacular is encouraged. *Conservative,* a middle path between Orthodox and Reform, accepts the binding nature of *Halakhah* but interprets it more liberally than Orthodox Judaism. It returned the use of Hebrew in worship (although not exclusively), a move echoed by late twentieth-century Reform Judaism. *Reconstructionist* sees Judaism as an evolving civilization. It has always retained more traditional ritual and practice than the Reform movement, but with deep reinterpretation. It rejects explicitly the traditional Jewish notion of "chosenness." *Humanistic* combines non-theistic philosophy and humanistic values with celebration of Jewish identity and culture, and recasts liturgies and celebrations accordingly. *Jewish Renewal* is a transdenominational movement rooted in Jewish mysticism.

To dig deeper: Kushner, Harold. *To Life! A Celebration of Jewish Being and Thinking.* Boston: Little, Brown and Company, 1993.

Native American Religion

This umbrella term for the beliefs, practices, and institutions of some five hundred fifty indigenous American societies with diverse languages, customs, and concepts of the divine includes the religions of particular nations such as Navajo, Keetoowah (Cherokee), or Lakota that have been reclaimed and continue to evolve. It also includes pan-Indian movements and associations that combine practices of many tribes and nations, and new religious movements such as the Native American Church. There is a rich oral tradition of sacred narratives and prayers, some of which are now in written form.

Beliefs: Broad generalities are difficult, but commonalities include a belief that everything has life, that all life has a spirit, and that all life is interconnected—which leads to a profound respect for the earth, plants, and animals. Most would affirm an essential monotheism with multiple realms of spiritual beings, and a certainty of life after death.

Practices: These may include agricultural and hunting rituals, ceremonies to honor passage from one stage of life to the next, use of totems, *shamanism* (use of spiritual specialists), and holistic approaches to healthcare.

To dig deeper: Martin, Joel W. *The Land Looks After Us: A History of Native American Religion.* New York: Oxford University Press, 2001.

Shinto

The original name for Japan's ancient indigenous natural religion is *kami-no-michi.* The name Shinto—from the Chinese *Shen-tao*—dates from the sixth century CE. Both mean "the way of the gods." Shinto has no canon of scriptures, but a colorful body of folk literature conveys basic beliefs, and several ancient collections of writings are deemed important.

Beliefs: Shinto-followers seek harmony with the *kami* (deities or spirits), manifest in natural phenomena, clan ancestors, and spirits of deceased emperors, saints, and heroes. Shinto maintains a positive attitude toward nature and life, but gives high priority to ritual purity. Pollution is believed to be caused by decay or bodily discharges (not moral guilt), and must be cleansed ritually. Human character and relationships must be kept healthy and pure. Shinto's esteem for nature speaks to today's ecological concerns.

Practices: Shinto practice includes worship at a public or home shrine, observing purification customs and the annual cycle of festivals. Some thirteen sects, dating from the nineteenth century, have their own characteristic practice style, and process for certifying priests.

To dig deeper: Ellwood, Robert S., and Richard Pilgrim. *Japanese Religion: A Cultural Perspective.* Englewood Cliffs, N.J.: Prentice-Hall, 1992.

Sikhism

Sikhism was founded by Guru Nanak (1469–1539) in Punjab, India. After his death, the community was led by a series of nine Gurus, the last of whom died in 1708. The fourth Guru founded the Golden Temple, Sikhism's holiest site, in the city of Amritsar (from which the Sikh Code of Conduct is set and administered). The fifth Guru organized Sikhism's holy book, the *Guru Granth Sahib,* which contains hymns and writings of the first five Gurus, along with hymns and writings of Hindu and Muslim saints. The tenth Guru established the *Khalsa* (Community of the Pure) and the ritual of initiation. All Sikhs are followers of the Sikh *Panth* (Way); all initiated Sikhs (women and men) are members of the *Khalsa,* and some define the term more broadly. Sikhism has no clergy; anyone may lead worship. In the United States, local *gurdwaras* (houses of worship) are autonomous institutions, but some networking has been developed. The vast majority of Sikhs are part of the religion's mainline. Members of the movement founded by Yogi Bhajan (Harbhajan Singh, 1929–2004), the primary vehicle of conversion to Sikhism in the United States, speak of themselves as followers of Sikh Dharma, a term not generally used by other Sikhs.

Beliefs: For Sikhs, God is One, personal, omnipotent, the immortal creator of all. Sikhism teaches the brotherhood of humanity, rejection of caste, and futility of idol-worship. The goal is *moksha* (liberation): release into God's love, thus into everlasting bliss. Sikhs believe that, shortly before his death, Guru Gobind Singh (the tenth Guru) declared that ultimate authority would henceforth reside in Sikhism's holy book, rather than in a human guru. The *Guru Granth Sahib* is therefore regarded as a living teacher and object of highest sanctity.

Practice: Sikhs are to worship God, earn an honest living, and serve humanity. Communal worship features congregational prayer-singing and takes place in a *gurdwara* (Door of the Guru), which can be any room or building in which the holy book is the central object and treated with reverence. Individual worship includes daily ritual prayers and remembrance of God's holy name. The Sikh Dharma movement adds *kundalini yoga* to traditional Sikh practices. Some Sikhs undergo a ritual initiation called "taking *amrit.*" Sikhs may wear one or more of the Five Ks (five articles of faith): unshorn hair (which men usually cover with a turban), comb, underwear, a ceremonial dagger, and a steel bracelet. Initiated Sikhs must wear these articles, and are to abstain from alcohol and tobacco. They add Singh (Lion) if male, and Kaur (Princess) if female, to their name.

To dig deeper: Singh, Jasprit. *Style of the Lion: The Sikhs.* Ann Arbor, Mich.: Akal Publications, 1998.

Taoism

The name "Taoism" arose to differentiate this ancient tradition from Confucianism. As an umbrella term, it holds together various longevity practices, a literary-philosophical tradition, and a plethora of sects that draw upon both. The *Tao-te Ching* (The Book of the Way and its Virtue) articulates Taoism's philosophical basis. Sectarian Taoism, dating from the second century CE, has a priesthood and ordained ascetics. It exists in the United States, but practice-groups are more common, and participants may not necessarily consider themselves "Taoists." Taoism has long been practiced in conjunction with Confucianism and Mahayana Buddhism as the Three Teachings.

Beliefs: Tao is the unnamed first-cause of the universe, a force that flows through all life. The goal is to become one with the Tao through *wu-wei* (actionless action)—that is, allowing nature to take its course. The *yin-yang* symbol, an important concept in Confucianism as well, expresses the core principle of "balance out of chaos." It represents the complementarity of opposites, and the virtue of holding opposites in balance.

Practice: Emphasis is on maintaining the harmony of the family. In order to align oneself with the *Tao,* one may practice *Tai-ch'i,* the cultivation of *ch'i* (inner energy) by means of a system of exercises, or *Ch'i-kung,* which promotes longevity and well-being by means of dynamic and static meditation postures. Folk Taoism involves many domestic rituals. Taoist practice may include ceremonial worship of deities (from the Jade Emperor to the Kitchen God), herbal medicine, *Feng Shui,* and more.

To dig deeper: Jochim, Christian. *Chinese Religions: A Cultural Perspective.* Englewood Cliffs, N.J.: Prentice-Hall, 1986.

Zoroastrianism

Also called Zarathustrianism, Zoroastrianism is the western name for "The Good Religion." It is based on the teachings of the Prophet Zarathustra ("Zoroaster" in Greek), who lived sometime between 1200 and 550 BCE, in what is now Iran. Zoroastrianism was the state religion during three eras of Persian/Iranian history. It has been a significant presence in India since the ninth century, where adherents are known as Parsis. The religion's conservative wing insists on the authority of the entire *Avesta* (collection of sacred texts). For "progressive" or "liberal" Zoroastrians, only the *Gathas* (hymns arguably dating from Zarathustra himself) have authority. American Zoroastrians divide on these theological-philosophical grounds, the two streams differing significantly in belief and practice. Additionally, they may fall informally into denominations according to which of several calendars govern their annual observances. American worship centers are autonomous, but some networking has been established.

Beliefs: Zoroastrians worship Ahura Mazda (Wise Lord), the one God. Ahura Mazda is the uncreated, immanent, and transcendent source of all that is good, true, and beautiful, for whom fire is the only appropriate symbol. Fire may also symbolize the divine spark within every person. The *Amesha Spentas* (Bountiful Immortals)—Discerning Mind, Righteousness, Benevolence, Good Power, Perfection, and Immortality—are divine attributes that are to be emulated by humanity in order to bring about the perfection of creation, which is the ultimate goal. For traditionalists, the twin Spirits, Spenta Mainyu and Angra Mainyu, represent the good force and the destructive force. They are in constant battle, but ultimately, good will triumph by Ahura Mazda's power. Humanity has innate freedom of will, and when all human will is in harmony with God's will, Angra Mainya will be conquered. Assistance in choosing the good comes from angelic beings (the *Yazatas)* and one's guardian spirit (one's *fravashi).*

Practices: Zoroastrians are to think good thoughts, speak good words, and do good deeds. The *Navjote* (the initiation rite) is the same for girls as for boys. Observant Zoroastrians pray five times daily in the presence of "clean" fire (symbol of God and of righteousness). The Zoroastrian priesthood is hereditary, and priests are necessary for the performance of the *Jashan* (the fire ceremony commemorating any important event).

To dig deeper: Boyce, Mary. *Zoroastrians: Their Religious Beliefs and Practices.* New York: Routledge, 2001.

FOR GENERAL READING

Eck, Diana. *A New Religious America: How a "Christian Country" Has Become the World's Most Religiously Diverse Nation.* San Francisco: Harper San Francisco, 2001.

Fisher, Mary Pat. *Living Religions,* sixth edition. Upper Saddle River, N.J.: Prentice-Hall, 2005.

Galanti, Geri-Ann. *Caring for Patients from Different Cultures,* third edition. Philadelphia: University of Pennsylvania Press, 2004.

Garces-Foley, Kathleen, ed. *Death and Religion in a Changing World.* Armonk, N.Y.: M. E. Sharpe, 2006.

Matlins, Stuart M., ed. *The Perfect Stranger's Guide to Funerals and Grieving Practices: A Guide to Etiquette in Other People's Religious Ceremonies.* Woodstock, Vt.: Skylight Paths Publishing, 2000.

GLOSSARY

Adanado (Cherokee): pronounced "a-DAH-nah-DOH"; the "heart" side of the human spirit. See *Udayvladv*.

Advaita (Hinduism): non-dualism; the notion that the human self and Ultimate Reality are of the same essence, with any difference we *perceive* being due to ignorance.

Ahimsa (Jainism): non-harm; doctrine of non-violence.

Ahura Mazda (Zoroastrianism): literally, Wise Lord; the most common name for God.

Amitabha (Buddhism): the Buddha of Boundless Light; also, *Amida Buddha*.

Amrit (Sikhism): nectar; sweetened water used for initiation; *amritdhari*, initiated Sikh.

Anatman, Anatta (Buddhism): no-self, in Sanskrit or Pali respectively.

Ani-yvwiya (Cherokee): principal people, or real people; name for the Cherokee People themselves; also, *yvwiya*: person.

Aparigraha (Jainism): the principle of non-attachment.

Ardas (Sikhism): petition; lengthy concluding prayer for congregational worship, also part of the individual daily evening prayer rites.

Arya-bodhisattva (Buddhism): see *bodhisattva*.

Arya Samaj (Hinduism): literally, Noble Society, a reform movement dating from 1876, which rejects use of images and traditional rituals in worship, and emphasizes social justice.

Asha (Zoroastrianism): ideal truth.

Ashé (Afro-Caribbean): life; things that represent life-force.

Asogwe (Afro-Caribbean): adjective denoting a Vodou priest of highest rank.

Atman (Hinduism, Sikhism): the true self underlying outward human appearance.

Avatar (Hinduism): the earthly manifestation of a deity.

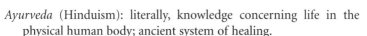

Ayurveda (Hinduism): literally, knowledge concerning life in the physical human body; ancient system of healing.

BAPS (Hinduism): acronym for *Bochasanwasi Shri Akshar Purushottam Swaminarayan Sanstha,* a movement whose members worship Swaminarayan, their founding teacher, as an *avatar* of Vishnu, thus God himself.

Bardo (Buddhism): Sanskrit for intermediate state; refers to the state between two earthly lives, during which a series of experiences, ranging from sublime to terrifying, offer opportunities for enlightenment; *Bardo Thodol:* so-called "Tibetan Book of the Dead," a classic text describing this series of experiences.

Barzakh (Islam): intermediate state; the period between the death of an individual and the general resurrection of all humanity.

Bhagavad-Gita (Hinduism): sixth book of the *Mahabharata* (a Hindu epic), in which Krishna teaches the path of spiritual progress.

Bhajan (Hinduism, Jainism, Sikhism): chant, song of praise.

Bhakti (Hindu): devotion; *bhakti yoga:* path of devotion.

Bikur cholim (Judaism): literally, visiting the sick; refers to individuals, groups, and organizations that perform the mitzvah of doing good deeds for someone who is ill.

Bodhisattva (Buddhism): one who achieves Nirvana, but refuses it in order to bring more beings to Enlightenment. *Arya-bodhisattva:* noble *bodhisattva.*

Byoki-heyu (Shinto): prayer for the healing of sickness.

Brahman (Hinduism): Ultimate Reality, the impersonal ultimate principle.

Brahmin (Hinduism): priestly class, the highest of the four traditional castes.

Chetna (Jainism, Hinduism): awareness, energy, spiritual energy.

Chevra kadisha (Judaism): literally, holy fellowship; a society of laypersons who prepare the body of the deceased for burial according to Jewish law.

Ching Ming (Taoism): literally, "clear and bright"; a spring festival for remembering one's ancestors by tending their graves.

Chinvat Bridge (Zoroastrianism): Bridge of the Separator; the soul's passageway after death; an instrument of judgment.

Darbe mehr (Zoroastrianism): literally, door of justice or door of peace; a Zoroastrian house of worship and community center.

Dana (Buddhism): giving; merit-making.

Dhammapada (Buddhism): literally, "Teaching of the Verses"; an important collection of 423 verses collected from discourses of the Buddha.

Dharma (Hinduism, Buddhism, Jainism): literally, upholding; in Pali dialect, *dhamma*. Hinduism: moral order, righteousness, religion; Buddhism: the teaching of Buddha, correct conduct for one's level of spiritual awareness. Jainism: the teaching of the *tirthankaras;* also, that which makes or encourages motion.

Didahnawisgi (Cherokee): pronounced "dee-DAHH-na-WISH-kee"; medicine priest; a traditional healer in the Cherokee (Keetoowah) tradition.

Diwali (Hinduism): Festival of Lights.

Dvaita (Hinduism): two-ness; dualism; the notions that all things are different from one another in essence, and the most difference is between God and the individual self.

Feng shui (Taoism): the practice of determining the most harmonious location.

Five Ks (Sikhism): five articles (markers) of faith worn by observant Sikhs: *kes* (unshorn hair covered with a turban or veil, and unshorn beard), *kangha* (comb), *kara* (steel bracelet), *kachh* (undershorts), and *kirpan* (dagger).

Frashokereti (Zoroastrianism): literally, making fresh, renovation; the process by which good is triumphant.

Fravashi (Zoroastrianism): the divine essence within each individual; the pure, incorruptible spiritual idea of each entity created by Ahurda Mazda; guardian spirit.

Ganesha (Hinduism): also, Ganesh; elephant-headed deity of wisdom and good fortune, the Remover of Obstacles, son of Parvati and Shiva; sometimes called Ganapati.

Gathas (Zoroastrianism): hymns of Zarathustra; earliest Zoroastrian sacred texts.

Gautama (Buddhism): the Buddha's family name.

Geshe (Buddhism): in Tibetan Buddhism, a professor or senior teacher; *Geshe-la:* a respectful means of referring to a senior teacher.

Gurbani (Sikhism): literally, utterance of the Guru; all or a portion of the contents of the *Guru Granth Sahib* (Holy Book).

Gurdwara (Sikhism): place for congregational worship in which the Sikh holy book is installed.

Guru (Hinduism, Sikhism): for Hindus, a teacher, usually an ascetic; for Sikhs, one of the historic inspired leaders of the community.

Guru Granth Sahib (Sikhism): the Sikh holy book.

Gutka (Sikhism): Prayer book.

Gwo-bon-zanj (Afro-Caribbean): in Haitian Kreyòl, "big good angel"—that is, the soul; sometimes, *gros-bon-ange.*

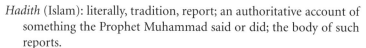

Hadith (Islam): literally, tradition, report; an authoritative account of something the Prophet Muhammad said or did; the body of such reports.

Hajj (Islam): pilgrimage to Mecca, made during a specific period of the Islamic year, and involving particular details of preparation and performance.

Halal (Islam): permissible, according to Islamic law.

Haram (Islam): prohibited, according to Islamic law.

Hare Krishna (Hindu): a member of the International Society of Krishna Consciousness (ISKCON), so called because the main devotional practice is the chanting of a mantra composed of these words.

Hatha yoga (Hinduism): literally, sun-moon path to God, the ritual discipline of breathing exercises and postures.

Haudenosaunee (Native American): pronounced "ho-den-no-SHO-nee"; the People of the Long House; the Iroquois Confederacy, of which the Cayuga, Mohawk, Oneida, Onondaga, Seneca, and Tuscarora Nations are members.

Houngan (Afro-Caribbean): Vodou male priest.

Houris (Islam): a common transliteration of the Arabic *hawra* (white ones), a term used in a number of early Qur'an verses to refer to female companions in the Hereafter.

Imam (Islam): leader, particularly of communal prayer; in Shi'ah Islam, one of a series of authoritative and divinely guided leaders of the entire community.

Itai (Shinto): the ongoing relationship between the deceased and the bereaved.

Janaazah (Islam): funeral; *salaat al-janaazah,* a special supplication to God on behalf of a Muslim who has died.

Jannah, al- (Islam): the Garden; Paradise.

Japji (Sikhism): a thirty-eight-stanza hymn composed by Guru Nanak that stands at the beginning of the *Guru Granth Sahib;* one of five hymns initiated Sikhs recite daily.

Jashan (Zoroastrianism): communal ceremony commemorating or celebrating an important occasion or event, performed by a priest and making use of a fire-urn.

Jiva (Jainism, Hinduism, Sikhism): the immortal essence of any living being.

Jizo Bodhisattva (Buddhism): Japanese version of Ksitigarbha (the Earth Store Bodhisattva), the guardian of children and travelers.

Jnana yoga (Hinduism): the path to God through study.

Jum'ah (Islam): literally, assembly; *Yaumu'l-Jum'ah:* Day of Assembly, Friday congregational prayer, held at midday.

Kaddish (Judaism): literally, holy (in Aramaic); doxology ending the individual sections of Jewish liturgy; *Mourner's Kaddish:* prayer said at the end of each service by close relatives of the deceased during the year following the death, and on the anniversary of the death.

Kami (Shinto): the extraordinary, the sacred, but also individual deities or spirits; used as plural as well as singular.

Karma (Hinduism, Buddhism, Jainism): for Hindus and Buddhists, moral law of cause and effect; for Jains, particle residue on one's soul from all of one's actions, both positive and negative.

Karma yoga (Hinduism): the path to God through action; the spiritual discipline of selfless service.

Keetoowah (Native American): Cherokee. While often used interchangeably, some members of this First Nation prefer to be called Keetoowah rather than Cherokee; others use Cherokee as a political designation, and Keetoowah to label their spiritual practice.

Kesadhari (Sikhism): One who has "kept" his or her hair; one whose hair is unshorn.

Kirpan (Sikhism): dagger, sword; one of the Five Ks.

Kirtan (Hinduism; Sikhism): devotional hymn-singing, often with instrumental accompaniment.

Kittel (Judaism): Yiddish for "gown"; the white burial garment.

Kosher (Judaism): in accord with the dietary requirements of Jewish law.

Kriav (Judaism): literally, "tearing," as in the ripping of one's garment upon the death of an immediate relative.

Krishna (Hinduism): an *avatar* of Vishnu.

Kuan-Yin (Buddhism): the one who hears the sound of the world; the *Bodhisattva* of Compassion as feminine. (In Vietnamese, *Quan Am.*)

Kushti (Zoroastrianism): sacred cord worn wrapped several times around the waist by initiated Zoroastrians, which is untied and retied during ritual daily prayer.

Lama (Buddhism): literally, Higher One; a Tibetan Buddhism monk, particularly recognized to be the reincarnation of a great spiritual teacher.

Langar (Sikhism): a free communal vegetarian meal at a *gurdwara*, served and eaten in a way that demonstrates the abolition of caste.

Lùkùmì (Afro-Caribbean): Afro-Cuban religion; also, Chango or Shango.

Lwa (Afro-Caribbean): in Vodou, spiritual entities, similar to *orisha* in other Afro-Caribbean religions.

Mahayana (Buddhism): literally, Great Vehicle; the northern stream of Buddhism.

Mala (Buddhism; Hinduism): prayer beads.

Manbo (Afro-Caribbean): from, "Keeper of the Medicinal Packet," a female Vodou priest; a man is *houngan;* in either case, a high priest adds the term *asogwe.*

Mandir (Hinduism): temple.

Mantra (Hinduism, Jainism, Buddhism, Sikhism): literally, an instrument of thought; a sound, word, or phrase (sometimes thought to be of divine origin) chanted to evoke the vibration of an aspect of creation, to focus meditation, or as an act of praise.

Mèt Tèt (Afro-Caribbean): Haitian Kreyòl term meaning "Master of One's Head"; that particular deity that is most significant for an individual Vodouisant.

Minyan (Judaism): quorum of ten adults necessary for Jewish communal worship; for Orthodox, men only.

Mi Sheberach (Judaism): a traditional prayer for healing, usually said after the Torah reading in synagogue services.

Mishnah (Judaism): the first compilation of the Oral Law; a compendium of legal opinion dating from approximately 200 BCE to 200 CE, organized under six broad headings (agriculture and tithing; Sabbath and holidays; family law, including marriage issues; civil and criminal law; rules concerning temple sacrifice; and ritual purity laws).

Mitama (Shinto): literally, dead soul.

Mitzvah (Judaism): commandment.

Moksha (Hinduism, Jainism): release, liberation (that is, from *samsara*—the cycle of rebirth); sometimes, *moksh;* in Punjabi, *mukti.*

Nahr, al- (Islam): the Fire; that is, eternal punishment.

Navkar Maha Mantra (Jainism): the Great Salutation Formula; Jainism's most important formula, also known as the *Pancha Namaskara* (the fivefold salutation) because it pays homage to the five categories of spiritual beings: the *arahants,* the *siddhas;* the living spiritual leaders, the teachers of the scriptures, and all renunciates.

Nembutsu (Buddhism): Japanese for "mindfulness of the Buddha"; the Pure Land practice of chanting, "I take refuge in the Amida Buddha"; in Chinese, *nien-fwo.*

Nirvana (Buddhism): cessation—of participation in *samsara,* the endless cycle of birth, death, and rebirth.

Norito (Shinto): prayer; sacred words said formally to the *kami* in ancient Japanese.

Obon (Buddhism): Japanese Buddhist Hungry Ghost Festival; a season celebrated by drumming, singing, and dancing. It includes the Floating Lantern Ceremony in memory of those who have died.

Omamori (Shinto): literally, protection; amulet to guard against misfortune.

Orisha (Afro-Caribbean): Yoruba for a deity; sometimes used to mean West African traditional religion in general.

Paket kongo (Afro-Caribbean): medicinal packets used for healing practices.

Pali (Buddhism): the Indian dialect in which the Buddha's teachings were first recorded.

Pancha mahabhuta (Hinduism): the five basic elements of the universe, or the five states of being of all matter—earth, fire, wind, water, and ether.

Panch Kalyanak Puja (Jainism): from *kalyank* (event), Five Events Worship; from a ceremony that recalls the Five Great Events in the life of Mahavira: conception, birth, renunciation, attainment of omniscience, achieving of *moksh.*

Parsi (Zoroastrianism): a member or descendant of the community of Zoroastrians in residence in India since the eighth century CE.

Péristyle (Afro-Caribbean): in Vodou, a temple's interior space, open to the public and distinguished by having a large tree that acts as a center-post.

Pesach (Judaism): Passover; the Feast of Unleavened Bread—an eight-day recollection of escape from slavery into freedom through divine intervention.

Pikuach nefesh (Judaism): literally, preservation of life; the obligation (and, when necessary, the suspension of all other laws) to protect and save life.

Puja (Hinduism, Buddhism, Jainism): literally, respect, homage; rituals of offering in which an image (of a deity, or the Buddha, or a *tirthankara*) is treated as an honored guest; *pujari*: a temple staff-member with special training for performing the daily rituals of offering and respect-paying.

Punjabi (Sikhism): the language of the region of northern India in which Sikhism emerged; people, things, customs from that region.

Purim (Judaism): holiday commemorating the heroism of Queen Esther on behalf of the Jewish people.

Qi (Taoism): pronounced "chee"; literally, breath; often translated as *energy.*

Qigong (Taoism): pronounced "chee-kung"; the modern term for the ancient tradition of Taoist alchemy (or, healing arts).

Quan Am (Buddhism): see *Kuan-Yin.*

Qur'an (Islam): God's direct revelation to the Prophet Muhammad in Arabic, now preserved in written form.

Rabbi (Judaism): teacher; synagogue leader. "The Rabbis" refers to the ancient sages whose opinions are cited in the Talmud, and/or who helped to codify Jewish scriptures as the *Tanakh*; "Rabbinic" refers to the era during which they lived.

Raja yoga (Hinduism): royal yoga, which features eight "limbs" or steps: abstinence, discipline, postures, breath-control, sense withdrawal, concentration, meditation, and *samadhi* (superconscious state of union with the divine).

Rosh ha-Shanah (Judaism): New Year; literally, head of the year.

Sacred thread (Hinduism): a knotted cord worn over one shoulder by twice-born Hindu boys and men (and some upper-caste girls and women) who have gone through a ceremony marking their transition to the student stage of life.

Salat (Islam): the obligatory prayer rite.

Samawat, al- (Islam): the heavens; that is, the cosmos. (See *al-Jannah.*)

Samsara (Hinduism, Jainism, Sikhism, Buddhism): the cycle of life, death, and rebirth.

Sanskrit (Hinduism): the classical language of Hindu scriptures.

Seder (Judaism): Hebrew for "order"; can refer to the order of prayers in a liturgy, the six major divisions of the Mishnah; or a ritual meal, as in the Passover *seder*—a meal that recalls the escape of the ancient Hebrews from slavery in Egypt.

Sensei (Buddhism, Shinto): Japanese for "teacher," a term of respect below the rank of *roshi,* used for martial arts instructors, Pure Land priests, and Zen priests.

Shabad (Sikhism): literally, "word"; a hymn from Sikh scripture.

Shabbat (Judaism): Seventh day of the Jewish week, observed from sundown Friday until an hour past sundown on Saturday, by worship and abstinence from work.

Shakyamuni (Buddhism): Alternate name for Siddhartha Gautama (the Buddha), which refers to his membership in the Shakya tribe.

Shari'ah (Islam): literally, "the broad path that leads to water;" Divine Law.

Shavuot (Judaism): Feast of Weeks; also called Pentecost.

Sheol (Judaism): in the Torah, a place the dead go for punishment or purification.

Shi'ah (Islam): branch of Islam whose members assert that Ali (the Prophet's son-in-law) should have succeeded Muhammad as leader of the Muslim community upon his death; it differs somewhat from Sunni Islam on theological and legal matters, and in certain details of practice.

Shin-jin (Buddhism): joyful faith; Japanese term for awareness of one's Buddha-nature.

Shivah (Judaism): seven; period of intense mourning for an immediate family-member.

Shmirah (Judaism): the *mitzvah* of keeping vigil over a corpse until its burial.

Shomer; shomera (Judaism): guard; one who keeps vigil over a corpse until its burial.

Siddhartha (Buddhism): the Buddha's given name; also, Siddhartha Gautama.

Siddur (Judaism): prayer book; specifically, a book of liturgies for Jewish services.

Simchat Torah (Judaism): literally, Joy of Torah; a celebration of the completion of the annual Torah lectionary.

Sloshim (Judaism): thirty; the first thirty days after the death of a family member, during which certain mourning practices are to be observed.

Sohila prayer (Sikhism): literally, Hymn of Joy; formal late evening prayer said at bedtime, when storing the scriptures for the night, and at cremation of the dead.

Son Buddhism (Buddhism): Korean Zen.

Soreisya (Shinto): ancestral deity.

Sudreh (Zoroastrianism): undergarment worn by initiated Zoroastrians.

Sukkot (Judaism): Feast of Booths or Tabernacles.

Sunni (Islam): follower of the Prophet's example; mainstream Islam.

Sutra (Buddhism): literally, thread; a collection of the Buddha's teachings.

Swastika (Jainism): sacred diagram of the four possible destinies of any life-form (embodiment as a heavenly, human, animal, or hellish being).

Tallit (Judaism): rectangular prayer shawl with tassels on each corner.

Talmud (Judaism): the authoritative compendium of rabbinical commentary on the Mishnah, including legal, ritual, theological, and ethical material.

Tanu (Zoroastrianism): the physical body.

Tao (Taoism, Confucianism): pronounced "dauw"; The Way, the path; for Taoism, the "unnamable," thus the metaphysical absolute, the way of passive acceptance and mystical contemplation; for Confucianism, the right way within the human world.

Tefillin (Judaism): black leather boxes worn on the head and left arm by observant adult male Jews during the weekday morning prayer ritual; also called *phylacteries*.

Tehillim (Judaism): psalms.

Theravada (Buddhism): literally, the Way of the Elders; the surviving expression of the earliest schools of Buddhism; sometimes called Hinayana (Lesser Vehicle).

Ti-bon-zanj (Afro-Caribbean): in Haitian Kreyòl, "little good angel"—that is, the aspects of rationality, intuition, and emotion; sometimes, *ti-bon-anj, ti-bon-ange*.

Tirthankara (Jainism): ford-maker, crossing-maker; someone capable of finding the way out of the endless cycle of life; one of twenty-four inspired teachers who appear during each eon to perform this function for humanity, Mahavira being the most recent.

Torah (Judaism): the Five Books of Moses; the Pentateuch; more broadly, the entirety of Jewish sacred texts.

Tsuya (Shinto): literally, "throughout the night"; an all-night vigil for the deceased.

Udayvladv (Native American): pronounced "oo-DAH-yuh-luh-DUH"; the Cherokee term for the "shadow" side of the human spirit. See *Adanado*.

Upanishads (Hinduism): a body of literature that completes the Vedas, and lays out key doctrines such as *karma, samsara,* and reincarnation.

Urvan (Zoroastrianism): the individuality, or soul.

Usvhiyi (Cherokee): pronounced "oo-SAH-hee-YEE"; the Cherokee term for the Darkening Land, the abode of the spirit after the death of the body.

Vedas (Hinduism): knowledge; ancient scriptures forming the basis of Hindu belief and practice; the *Rig Veda* is the oldest of these collections.

Vihara (Buddhism): monastery (Sri Lankan Theravada term).

Vishishta Advaita (Hinduism): qualified non-dualism.

Vishnu (Hinduism): Ultimate Reality itself, incarnating repeatedly for the sake of the material world; or, Personal Sustainer aspect of Ultimate Reality, thus preserver of the universe.

Vodouisant (Afro-Caribbean): an adherent of Vodou (Afro-Haitian religion); in Kreyòl, *Vodouwizan*.

Wake-mitama (Shinto): a portion of a spiritual entity.

Won Buddhism (Buddhism): from "won" (circular), a Korean movement dating from 1915, which combines elements of Theravada, Pure Land, and Zen understandings and practices.

Worldview (All): the constellation of doctrines, narratives, rituals or practices, ethical or legal understandings, and institutions by which one makes sense of the world.

Yajna (Hinduism): fire sacrifice.

Yin-yang (Taoism, Confucianism): balance out of chaos; the complementarity and necessity of opposites.

Yoga (Hinduism): ancient path or method for attaining release from *samsara*.

Yom Kippur (Judaism): Day of Atonement; high point of the Jewish year, observed with a twenty-four-hour fast and seeking forgiveness from one's neighbors and associates.

Yoruba (Afro-Caribbean): referring to the religion of people of this language-group from Western Africa (particularly, Nigeria).

Zabihah (Islam): slaughtering of animals according to Islamic law.

Zendo (Buddhism): a hall in which *zazen* (sitting meditation, the primary practice of Zen Buddhism) is practiced.